Refreshingly Simple
Finance
for Small Business

eBook edition

As a buyer of the print edition of *Refreshingly Simple Finance for Small Business* you can now download the eBook edition free of charge to read on an eBook reader, your smartphone or your computer. Simply go to:

http://ebooks.harriman-house.com/finance

or point your smartphone at the QRC below.

You can then register and download your eBook copy of this book.

www.harriman-house.com

Refreshingly Simple
Finance
for Small Business

A straight-talking guide to finance and accounting

Emily Coltman ACA

Enterprise Nation

An Enterprise Nation Book
www.enterprisenation.com

HARRIMAN HOUSE LTD
3A Penns Road
Petersfield
Hampshire
GU32 2EW
GREAT BRITAIN

Tel: +44 (0)1730 233870
Email: enquiries@harriman-house.com
Website: www.harriman-house.com

First published in Great Britain in 2012 by Harriman House, this revised edition published in 2013.

ISBN: 978-1-908003-20-1

British Library Cataloguing in Publication Data

A CIP catalogue record for this book can be obtained from the British Library.

Printed and bound in Great Britain by Marston Book Services Limited, Oxfordshire.

This book is for my Mum and Dad, who have supported me so much all my life, with a special hat tip to Dad who taught me to write and research.

Contents

Acknowledgements ix

About the Author xi

Introduction xiii

Chapter 1 – How should you set up and structure your business? 1

Chapter 2 – Where's the initial money coming from? 15

Chapter 3 – The paperwork 25

Chapter 4 – Simple accounts 35

Chapter 5 – Tax 61

Chapter 6 – Do I need an accountant? 91

Chapter 7 – Planning for the future 97

The End 107

Bibliography 109

Other Products from Enterprise Nation 110

Get the Best Support for Your Small Business 112

Acknowledgements

There are some very special people who've been supportive and inspirational to me in my career so far, and I'm delighted to be able to thank them here:

The whole team at FreeAgent, terrific colleagues and friends all of them. A special thank you to Kevin McCallum and Roseann Wilson for reviewing chapters of this book. Fudge doughnuts are on me!

All the great 2000-2007 team at Cannon Moorcroft, where I first discovered small business accounting. A special thank you to Michael Jeffries, who first taught me the importance of looking above and beyond the numbers. Have a KitKat!

My network of good friends from the business, accounting and software worlds, including, but not limited to, Richard Anning and all in the IT Faculty committee, Elaine Clark, Glen Feechan, Jason Holden, Robert Killington, Mark Lee, Richard Murphy, Adrian Pearson, Cally Robson, Phil Richards, Hugh Williams, Michael Wood and his team, Philip Woodgate, and Alan Young.

Special thanks here to Dennis Howlett, who first encouraged me to blog about accounting, and guided me through setting up my first business.

Special thanks also to Michael Green, who always seems to find time in a frenetic schedule to give me advice and encouragement just when I need it most. You're a star!

Emma Jones, who besides being an amazing small business champion also gave me the chance to write this book.

For case studies from real-life small businesses:

Vicky Duffield of Tots Teas, John O'Nolan, freelance interactive designer, and Ingrid Savill of Reecovid.

All my fantastic family and especially my wonderful husband Matthew, whose love, warmth and care are unstinting. Thank you so much, sweetheart.

About the Author

Emily Coltman, Chief Accountant to FreeAgent, is a very unusual Chartered Accountant – she speaks plain English as well as accounting-speak!

After graduating from the University of Cambridge, she trained and qualified with growing accountancy practice Cannon Moorcroft, where she looked after accounts and tax for a portfolio of micro-business clients.

This gave her a keen interest in accounting software and training, which led to starting up her own business making screen-capture tutorial videos, and later to joining FreeAgent, where she works with worldwide small businesses to help them use this simple online accounting system to keep their books in real time.

Emily is passionate about helping the owners of small and growing businesses to escape their fear of 'the numbers', and believes that, with the right tools and guidance – some of which she aims to provide in this book – absolutely anyone, even if they were hopeless at maths at school, can learn to look after the finances of a small business.

Introduction

This book is for all current and would-be small business owners who find that the idea of the whole financial and accounts side of running a business has them – literally or figuratively – running for the hills.

I have good news for you.

Even if you were hopeless at maths at school, you CAN do the finances.

Yes, you can.

Promise!

There are lots of tools out there to help you and in this book I'll illustrate some of the most useful for you. I'll also explain how you'll fit into the UK's tax system, which is overseen by HM Revenue & Customs (**www.hmrc.gov.uk**). That's a bit of a mouthful, so I've referred to them as HMRC in this book.

The UK's tax system[1] is something of a wilderness. This book is your map and compass.

And you don't need to know double-entry bookkeeping. I'm not even going to go there in this book!

When you're thinking how to organise your business's books, there's one question to always keep in your mind. The $64,000,000 question:

Why are you in business?

For example:

- Do you have a hobby that you love doing? You don't want to give up your day job but you could – or do – make a bit of money from your hobby? There are lots of people who do this.

---

[1] Where we look at business law, such as for business structure, it's the law as applies in England and Wales that we'll use.

True story

I have a friend from university who's a geological engineer by profession, but he's also an excellent Highland piper. He's in great demand to play at Burns Suppers, New Year's Eve parties, weddings and so forth, and he earns additional money by doing that. According to HMRC, that's a business, so he does have to record his finances and pay a bit of tax on that income.

- Do you want your business to just earn enough to keep your home and your family going, but no more than that? Some authors call this a lifestyle business.

- Would you like your business to grow big enough to take on 5, 10 or 20 staff?

- Can you see yourself as the next Richard Branson (OK, if you're a woman the beard might be a problem here) with a global empire?

Remember, all these are valid business choices. Don't believe the doomsayers who say that a hobby business, or lifestyle business, is not a real business. I've had a lifestyle business, so I can say with my hand on my heart, it is very much a real business!

The question of why you're in business will affect all your business decisions, but perhaps financing most of all, because you'll need to consider:

- How should I set up my business in terms of tax?

- What funding will my business need?

- How should I price the goods or services that my business sells?

- What records must I keep for my business?

- Do I need an accountant?

- How should I plan for my business's future?

Your reason for starting the business will affect all of these. Let's start by looking at how you might set up your business in terms of tax.

Chapter 1.

How should you set up and structure your business?

Remember the big question: why am I in business?

If you have a hobby business, or your priority is to keep your records as simply as you possibly can, or if you're worried that you might fall foul of tax traps, you might want to go for the simplest set-up available.

But if you feel more confident, your business is larger, and/or you want to (legally!) pay as little tax as possible, you might want to structure your business differently.

In the UK, there are four different ways you can set up your business for tax:

1. Sole trader

2. Partnership

3. Limited Liability Partnership (LLP)

4. Limited company

Let's have a look at what each of these means.

1. Sole trader

This is the simplest structure available and it's for businesses where only one individual is running the business. So if it's just you, your computer and your dogs (who don't count as business partners even if you're going to spend most of the profits on feeding them), then this could be for you.

As Wendy Pascoe puts it, "you wake up one morning and decide to start selling cut flowers from the bottom of your garden. That's it: you're now a sole trader".[2]

The advantages of being a sole trader are:

- The business is simple to set up and simple to run.

- There's nowhere near as much mandatory paperwork as is required for any of the other business structures.

- You don't have to put your address on any of your business documents except the invoices you issue to your customers, which helps keep your details private, especially if you're working from home.

- When you're working out your business's tax, if your business makes a loss in its first few years of trading you can set those losses off against your other income in current or previous years. This means you may get an upfront tax refund, which would help with your business's cashflow.

- You may also be able to take advantage of the simplified accounting method which is available from April 2013 and can make preparing your accounts more straightforward.

But there are disadvantages to being a sole trader:

- Legally, there's no difference between you and your business. You are the business. So if the business is sued, you're sued –

---

[2] *Starting a Business in the Country* by Wendy Pascoe (How To Books Ltd, 2005).

which means, in the absolutely worst-case scenario, that you could be at risk of losing your home, your car, and other personal belongings.

- Being in business on your own can be isolating. Make sure you have a good network out there. The web is a good place to start – check out sites like Enterprise Nation (**www.enterprisenation.com**) and UK Business Forums (**www.ukbusinessforums.co.uk/forums**).

  And do think about getting yourself a mentor to bounce ideas off.

- As a sole trader you can also pay more tax than you would if you ran your business through a limited company.

Who must I tell that I'm a sole trader?

You must tell HMRC that you are in business and you can do this online here: **online.hmrc.gov.uk/registration/newbusiness/introduction**. You must do this by 5th October after the end of the tax year in which you started your business, so if you started your business between 6th April 2012 and 5th April 2013, you'll need to register by 5th October 2013.

HMRC then require you to fill in a self-assessment tax return (often just called a tax return) every year. See chapter 5 for more information about these.

And that's it. You don't have to tell any other official agencies. If you need to register your business for VAT, which we'll look at in more detail in chapter 5 too, then you can do that at the same time as registering your business.

What taxes do I pay as a sole trader?

You'll pay income tax and class 4 National Insurance on the profits your business makes.

It's similar to having income tax and National Insurance deducted from your salary when you're an employee. However, when you're a sole trader you only pay tax and NI twice a year. More about that again in chapter 5 (I know I keep sending you there).

Unless your business is very small (its profits are under £5,725 in the 2013/14 tax year[3]), you'll also have to pay class 2 National Insurance, which is charged at a flat rate per week and doesn't vary with the amount of profit your business makes. In the 2013/14 tax year the rate is £2.70 a week and this is usually paid by direct debit, on a six-monthly basis.

Is a sole trader self-employed?

Yes. A freelancer isn't necessarily a sole trader, though. Some freelancers run their own limited companies.

2. Partnership

A partnership is just like a sole trader, except there is more than one individual running it, each partner must register with HMRC and one partner must register the partnership too.

Partnerships are taxed in the same way as sole traders, with each partner paying tax and class 4 NI on his/her share of the profits, and each partner being liable for class 2 NI. More about this in chapter 5.

---

[3] See chapter 5 for more about tax years.

There are some additional advantages to being in partnership, over and above being a sole trader:

- You'll have someone to share your business worries and triumphs with. Don't underestimate this!

- You can either choose a partner whose business strengths match yours or whose strengths complement yours.

- By having more than one of you working in the business you should be able to earn more money to cover the costs.

But there are some disadvantages to being in partnership:

- In legal terms, partners are what's called "jointly and severally liable" for the business and its debts. What that means in plain English is that if one partner steals the business's cash, the other partner(s) are still liable for the business's debts. And, just like a sole trader, legally there's no separation between the business and the partners, so partners could lose their homes, cars, etc.

- You and your partner(s) may want to take the business in different directions. For example, one might want to be the next Richard Branson, and the other might want a small business that won't grow beyond the kitchen table. Have a good chat about this and be frank with each other before you start your business. Better to not start at all than fall out later and wreck the business.

I can't stress enough that if you're going into partnership you must always, always, draw up a partnership agreement. That holds true even if you're going into business with your spouse or your best friend. You never know what might crop up when you're in business.

The partnership agreement should include:

- How much money each partner will put in, both for the initial start-up costs and for ongoing funding if the business runs short of cash.

- How much money each partner will take out, and when (each month, each year, every 5 years or so). When you're in partnership, as when you're a sole trader, there are no tax consequences for how you take money out of the business.

- The process for resolving any disputes. They will happen. Believe me, they will. No, honestly.

- What action will be taken if a partner leaves the business, or dies.

- The taking on of new partners: under what circumstances, if any, would you do this? How much cash would each new partner be required to put into the business, and how much could they take out on an ongoing basis?

- The expected retirement age of each of the partners. Remember, this may vary between partners. Does one partner want to keep working till they drop, and the other partner want to retire at 50 to their villa in the South of France? What would happen if one partner fell ill, or had a serious accident, and needed to retire early?

- How should the profit be divided between the partners? Most often the split is 50:50 but it doesn't have to be. Should the partner that puts in more cash, or does more work, be entitled to more of the profit?

- What will happen if one partner wants to close or sell the business and the other partners want to keep going. Whose decision will be final?

You can find template partnership agreements on various sites such as Partnership Agreement (**www.partnership-agreement.co.uk**). For extra protection, speak to a solicitor to make sure your agreement covers everything you need.

3. Limited Liability Partnership (LLP)

This is like a partnership (that is, more than one person owns it) but, as its name suggests, the liability of the partners is limited.

That means that, rather than the partners' own personal assets being at risk if the business is sued, they only have to pay out as much as they've put into the business.

An LLP, unlike an ordinary partnership, is a legal entity in its own right. That means it has its own identity separate from that of the people who own it. If the business is sued, it's the LLP that's sued not the partners – unless the partners have personally been guilty of wrongdoing.

LLPs are very common in some industries, for example firms of solicitors and accountants are often set up as LLPs. But in most business sectors they are quite rare.

An LLP is taxed just like a partnership so must be registered with HMRC in the same way.

If you turn your partnership into an LLP you get the advantage of limited liability, but the disadvantages are:

- An LLP must register with Companies House (**www.companieshouse.gov.uk**) because it's a separate legal entity. Companies House is a government body that keeps details of all LLPs and limited companies in the UK, including their names, registered addresses, who owns them, and their accounts.

- LLPs must file accounts every year at Companies House, which anyone can download and view for the cost of a few pounds. There's no keeping your figures private. There is, though, the option to file a short version of your accounts. These are called "abbreviated accounts".

- LLPs must publish their registered address on their website and any correspondence issued by the LLP, which includes emails.

- There's other paperwork to file too, such as an annual return, which gives information about who's involved in the LLP, and again this is available for download from Companies House by anyone who cares to pay for it.

- The rarity of the LLP means that, if you have an accountant, they might struggle with preparing your accounts – and if your accountant charges by the hour[4], they may charge you more for their extra hassle!

- Because an LLP is taxed like a partnership, if it makes losses in its early years, the partners can potentially claim a tax refund if they've paid tax on other income such as employment income. This is also available to sole traders and partners, but the beauty of the LLP is that it comes coupled with the protection of limited liability.

- LLPs cannot use the simplified accounting method.

4. Limited company

This is a very popular structure for small businesses in the UK, but it won't suit everyone.

You can tell if a small business is a limited company because its name will nearly always end in "Limited", "LTD", or "Ltd".[5]

A limited company doesn't have to have more than one individual involved in running it. It must, however, have one or more directors, who typically run the business on a day-to-day basis, and one or more shareholders, who own the business. These may be the same people. A lot of small companies only have one

---

[4] Be very careful if you choose an accountant who charges by the hour, as your bills can mount up very quickly, and you might find yourself paying for a trainee accountant to practice on your books! See chapter 6.

[5] This is for a private limited company, i.e. the shares can't be sold on the open market. A company whose shares can be bought and sold on the open market is called a "public limited company" and its name will end in plc. The rules for a plc are so complex that I'm not even going to try and go there in this book.

director and one shareholder – the same individual. That's perfectly OK.

Like an LLP, a limited company has its own legal identity. You and your business are not legally the same, even though you may be the only director and shareholder. That means that not all the money the company earns belongs to you.

The company is an employer, and you are not self-employed – you are an employee.

That can be an important distinction for tax, for example when you come to include costs such as training in your accounts.

The advantages of running your business through a limited company are:

- You get the protection of limited liability. Just like an LLP, you personally can't be sued for more than you've put into the business, unless you're found guilty of wrongdoing, in which case both you and the company could be sued.

- The tax the company pays on its profits (corporation tax), plus the income tax you pay on your earnings from the company, often comes to less than the tax and National Insurance you'd pay as a sole trader.

But the disadvantages are:

- Lack of privacy. You have to publish your company's name, registered number and full postal address on any correspondence issued by the company, and that includes emails and on your website.

- Like an LLP, limited companies must also file extra paperwork, such as accounts and an annual return at Companies House.

- Limited companies also have to file their own tax returns for corporation tax, as well as a self-assessment tax return for each of the directors.

- A limited company is a much more complex structure and it does come with quite a lot of tax pitfalls. One of these is that you have to be very careful indeed when you take money out of the company. The company can pay you a salary as a director, it can pay dividends on your shares if you're a shareholder and it has enough profit, and it can pay you back for any money you've put into the company, including money you spent personally on company costs (e.g. you buy a box of notepaper using cash out of your own back pocket). That's it! A lot of small company owners have problems distinguishing their money from the company's; you do have to be careful here, as taking out too much money from the company can mean extra tax to pay.

- You might also be asked to personally guarantee agreements such as rent agreements, if you have to lease office space. Be careful, as you could, in the very worst case, be at risk of losing your home and car and other personal assets in this situation, if your business fails.

- If your business makes losses in its first few years of trading, those losses can't be used to claim a refund of any income tax you've paid on other income, such as a salary you earned before starting the company.

- Limited companies really do need an accountant.

  Here's what another accountant says:

  "If you are running a limited company please get yourself an accountant at the earliest opportunity. This isn't a desperate measure to drum up business for my profession. It comes from frustration at seeing decent hardworking people getting very stressed and spending a lot of time trying to deal with and submit their own limited company accounts – often with expensive consequences in terms of late filing fees and poor practices."[6]

- Directors can be disqualified or go to prison if found guilty of wrongdoing.

---

[6] James Smith BSc ACA, *Keeping it Simple: Small Business Bookkeeping, Cash Flow, Tax and VAT*, ISBN 978-1-907302-16-9 (Taxcafe UK Ltd).

Who must I tell that I want to set up a limited company?

You must register, or "incorporate", the company at Companies House (**www.companieshouse.gov.uk**) and you can either do this directly, or by using a formation agent, who will collect your company information such as the company's and the directors' names, and register the company on your behalf.

The company must file corporation tax returns each year and pay corporation tax on its profits, so you must tell HMRC that a new company has been set up. You do that on HMRC's website. Go to **www.hmrc.gov.uk** and click Register at the top left, then follow the instructions.

And, because the company is an employer and you are an employee, you must register the company as an employer for PAYE (Pay as You Earn) which you can do at the same time as registering for corporation tax. PAYE is the tax that must be deducted from employees' salaries and paid to HMRC by their employers. A good accountant will take care of all this for you.

I'd like to finish this chapter by looking at another setup question:

Does your business need its own bank account?

If you're a sole trader running a hobby business, you may not need to set up a separate business account, and just use your personal bank account.

Be careful though. HMRC say that you must be able to distinguish between your own transactions and your business's when it comes to preparing your tax returns. So if either you personally, or your business, has a lot of transactions (for example, you are a jeweller and you make lots of small items for lots of different customers), then you may be well advised to have a separate bank account for your business.

My recommendation would be that every other business type should have a separate bank account. For a partnership or an LLP there is more than one person involved, so you need to be able to keep track of what belongs to the business, so that you know what belongs to each person. You might also want to vary how much access different people have to the bank account, and make limits on how much each person can withdraw. Different banks have different procedures for authorising this. Limited companies and LLPs need to have their own bank accounts because they are separate legal entities in their own right.

Many banks do offer free trading for start-up businesses for a year or two.

Warning!

Watch out for hidden charges after the free period. For example, some banks say that if you don't put £x into the account each month, you'll be charged an "admin fee". Read the small print and ask the question! There might also be charges per transaction on a business account, particularly in the case of cheques paid out.

Make sure you're comfortable with the bank you choose; you might need their help in the future so be sure to find a bank who understands and supports your business and is helpful. Don't necessarily go with the same bank your personal account is with. Shop around and make use of recommendations.

Once you've set up your bank account, use it! Try, if at all possible, to only use your business account for business transactions, and avoid paying for business transactions personally. So if you can avoid it, don't pay for your weekly shopping using your business debit card, and don't buy business stationery on a personal credit card. Remember, HMRC say you need to be able to distinguish between your business and personal transactions.

If you're going to take payment by credit card, you can either look at setting up a merchant account with your bank, in addition to your everyday business bank account, or you can use an online payment system such as PayPal (**www.paypal.com**) or Google Checkout (**checkout.google.com**). These are free to sign up to, but they have to make their money somehow and they do that by taking a percentage of your sales as a fee. The more money you make, the smaller the percentage.

There are also options to take payment by credit card on the move via your smartphone. Check out mPowa (**www.mpowa.com**) or iZettle (**www.izettle.comb**) if you make sales away from your office, for example at trade fairs or exhibitions, and would like to be able to take payment by credit card without having to take a merchant terminal. PayPal are also about to launch this service in the UK at the time of writing.

If you'd like to take payment by direct debit, have a look at GoCardless (**wwwgo.cardless.com**) which is a very quick way to set up direct debit collection.

***

Do think carefully about why you're in business before you choose a structure – and don't let the tax tail wag the business dog. You may well pay less tax if you opt for a limited company, but if your business is a hobby business, or if you're worried about the additional paperwork a limited company involves, you'd be well advised to keep it simple and be a sole trader, or a partnership if there are more than one of you.

Chapter 2.

Where's the initial money coming from?

You may not need much money to start up your business. Some businesses can be started for less than £500 and that includes the cost of a bottle of bubbly to celebrate![7]

What costs should I consider when starting a business?

There will be initial and ongoing costs to meet, such as having business cards and letterheads printed, and designing and hosting your website, probably before you start earning any money. And unless your business is a hobby, or you're keeping your day job and running a business in your spare time, you may also need to find some extra funds to run your home and feed your family until your business is on its feet.

Some businesses, such as pubs, need more money for start-up costs than others, because they need to buy in stock and rent premises before the first customer even sees the door, never mind walks through it. Whereas, if you're a freelance writer then you may well only need to buy a laptop, if you don't already have one, and wireless broadband, if you don't already have it installed.

---

[7] Emma Jones, *Spare Room Start Up: How to Start a Business from Home*, ISBN 978-1-905641-68-0 (Harriman House, 2008).

Buying equipment

Your business's start-up costs may include buying large items of equipment, for example a pub might need to buy new ovens, or fit out a room for cold storage for food and beer.

If your business needs equipment, consider buying it on hire purchase to avoid having to lay out a lot of money all at once. But make sure you read the small print of your hire purchase agreement. How much will you actually pay in the end? Is the rate of interest heinously high? If you're buying a particularly expensive item, does the lender want security (e.g. your home) which could be at risk if you default on the loan? Some agreements do also continue unless you specifically stop them, or buy the asset, so read the small print!

Alternatively, it may well be possible to buy some equipment second-hand, either from websites such as eBay (**www.ebay.co.uk**) or Gumtree (**www.gumtree.com**), or from business contacts. You can still claim tax relief on the cost of equipment that's not bought new.

True story

My husband's work gave me a second-hand PC when they no longer needed it, in exchange for a £25 donation to Cumbria Air Ambulance.

But do watch out for old computer equipment, because in some cases, a second- or third-hand computer may have an old operating system that current programmes may not work on, or may be out of date for anti-virus software. It may also need expensive or rare cartridges and replacement cables, and might not talk to other, more modern equipment.

True story

I thought I'd found a great bargain once with a second-hand printer costing £100, until I realised that the printer had no USB port and so couldn't talk to my new laptop.

So where should the money come from to fund your equipment, and to pay your business costs – and potentially also household costs – until your business is on its feet?

I wouldn't recommend you use your credit card to buy much of what you need for your business. I've seen business owners let this spiral out of control and then it's very hard to get back out of debt.

> ## Tip
>
> If you need to borrow money, get a copy of your credit record from Experian (**www.experian.co.uk**) and check it carefully for adverse entries, because they might be wrong or fraudulent. Banks and lenders will check your credit record and if there are adverse entries on it, you'll have a very difficult job trying to get them to lend you money.

Let's look at each of the different options for finding some extra cash.

Redundancy pay and/or savings

If you have savings, or redundancy pay, available to spend, you could use this in your business.

This is probably the simplest way to get your hands on extra cash. After all, it's already yours, there's no risk of not being able to pay it back (you'd hardly sue yourself), and you won't damage a relationship with a friend or family member if you don't pay them back. Your other personal assets, such as your home or car, also won't be at risk. You also won't have to give anyone else a stake in your business.

But the disadvantages are that you won't have that money to spend anywhere else, so you might have to postpone that dream holiday, or having your house redecorated. Plus, if your business fails, that money is gone. So you might want to put a proportion of your savings into a business and keep the rest aside for a rainy day.

If you don't have any savings, or don't want to spend them on your business, where else might you get the cash?

Family and friends

You could ask family members or wealthy friends to lend you the money.

The advantages of this are:

- It's very simple. There are no complicated agreements to work through, although you should agree how you're going to repay the loan – and put this in writing.
- Your family and friends won't have to run a credit check on you.
- Your family and friends may have valuable experience to share, particularly if they've run businesses of their own.
- You're very unlikely to be charged punitive interest.
- You're very unlikely (unless your family and friends are feeling very vindictive) to lose your home or other assets if you don't pay it back.

But there are definite disadvantages:

- It may potentially damage relationships, especially if the money doesn't get paid back.
- Your family and friends may want a stake in your business (shares for a limited company, to be a partner in a partnership) – and you may not want to give this to them.
- Your family and friends may want a share of your business's profits as well as getting their investment back.
- Your family and friends may want a say in how your business is run and what it does. This can cause arguments!

So the next alternative is a more independent one.

Bank

You could approach a bank to lend you the money.

Banks can provide either extra cash for your business's day-to-day running costs by way of an overdraft, or a one-off injection to help you start your business or buy new equipment, through a loan.

> ## Tip
>
> Negotiate an overdraft facility with your bank upfront, even if you don't think you'll need it – though do be aware you could be charged a fee. Banks charge considerably lower interest for authorised overdrafts as opposed to unauthorised ones.

What are the advantages of borrowing from the bank?

- It's kept on a strictly commercial footing.

- You don't risk savings or family relationships if you don't pay the money back.

- It's easy to keep track of where you are because especially for loans, the bank will make sure you have a fixed payment plan, so that both you and they can monitor what you owe. Check your statements carefully though, because banks can make mistakes too!

And what potential disadvantages should you bear in mind?

- The bank will want to see your detailed business plan, so you will have to prepare one. This might be overkill if you have a hobby business.

- The bank may want security against the loan and if your business has no assets, they may want to secure the loan against personal assets such as your home, which could be at risk if you can't make the repayments.

- You have to meet the monthly payments so be sure that you can earn enough to do so.

- You will have to pay interest for the term of the loan and this could be high.

- Technically the bank can call in its money on demand, so check the paperwork carefully.

- Also be aware that the bank may want you to take out loan protection insurance (theirs or a third party's) which increases your costs.

True story

I knew a bank manager who had to visit a mother whose son had just been killed in a motorcycle crash. Not to offer condolences, but because the loan the young man had taken out on the bike hadn't been protected with insurance; the bank manager had to ask the bereaved mother to make arrangements for repaying the loan.

But that said, loan protection insurance can be very expensive, and there are mixed views on how useful it is.

Always read the small print when you borrow money!

Angel investor or venture capital fund

Larger and more established businesses might look to borrow money from a business angel, or a venture capital fund. This route is also more suitable for limited companies, because the investor is almost certain to want shares in the business in return for their money.

Angels tend to be wealthy individuals with an interest in business generally or in your sector. Venture capital funds tend to be run by large organisations that want to invest in smaller businesses.

If you're looking for a business angel, try one of the following websites:

- Angel Investment Network
  (**www.angelinvestmentnetwork.co.uk**)
- Angels Den (**www.angelsden.com**)
- British Business Angels Association (**www.bbaa.org.uk**)
- Company Partners (**www.companypartners.com**)

Why would you want to opt to borrow money from a business angel or venture capital fund?

- You have the chance to build a commercial relationship with a knowledgeable, well-connected individual who can do a lot of good for your business, by providing advice and helping you make contacts.
- It's kept on a commercial footing.
- Business angels will not normally ask for security such as banks will, for example a business angel will not expect you to sell your home to repay them if your business fails.
- You don't risk savings or family relationships.

What are the disadvantages of this route?

- The investor will almost certainly want a stake in your business, so you'll no longer own it completely, and you'll have to give them some of the profits, because they will want to see their investment repaid and more, over time
- The investor may want to have a say in how you run your business and what you do. This may not square with what you want to do.

Other sources of funding

You could also look for grants that are available locally, or nationally, for your particular line of business.

There's a lot of information about grants on the web. Check out GRANTnet (**www.grantnet.com**), the grant section of Smarta (**www.smarta.com/advice/business-finance/small-business-grants/how-to-win-a-grant**), and, if you're looking to make your business more environmentally friendly, The Green Grants Machine (**www.greengrantsmachine.co.uk**).

> **True story**
>
> Ingrid Savill's business, Reecovid (**www.reecovid.co.uk**), creates funky paper products using waste material saved from landfill. Because her business is based in Scotland, Ingrid was eligible for a grant from Starter for 6, through the Cultural Enterprise Office, which helped fund her start-up costs (**www.culturalenterpriseoffice.co.uk/starterfor6**).

The Prince's Trust Enterprise Programme (**www.princes-trust.org.uk/enterprise_programme**) helps unemployed young people aged 16-30 (25 in Scotland) to start a business, and part of this is start-up funding. If you're eligible, it's worth applying.

You could also try the Enterprise Finance Guarantee (**www.bis.gov.uk/efg**) if you're finding it difficult to borrow money because you don't have security to offer.

Crowdfunding is an increasingly popular way for small businesses to find funds. You can register with a crowdfunding site such as Crowdcube (**www.crowdcube.com**) or Kickstarter (**www.kickstarter.com**) or Crowdfunder (**www.crowdfunder.co.uk**) Both these latter sites are aimed at creative businesses. You can then offer a gift, small or large, or perhaps free access to your business's services for a certain period of time, in return for funding. The beauty of this is that individual investors only have to pay a small amount each, and you don't have to give up shares in your business unless you want to. The Crowdcube site is for business owners who want to sell shares in their business, so choose your crowdfunding option carefully.

And one other alternative, once your business gets going, is to use a factoring provider, who will collect your sales income from your customers and pay it on to you, taking a percentage as their fees. This guarantees your income if you're worried that your customers might not pay you in good time, but means you do collect less overall. Again, read the factoring agreement carefully and ensure you fully understand the terms.

If you need more money for your business then you have to spare, consider carefully where this will come from. You have to decide which option is the most appropriate for you and your business.

Chapter 3.

The paperwork

When you're in business, no matter how small your business is, there will be a forest's worth of paperwork, and most of that will be generated by the financial side!

In this chapter we'll look at the records HMRC and other legal bodies require you to keep, and for how long. I'll give you some guidance as to what paper records you'll need to keep so that you can fulfil your legal obligations, and I'll also give you some suggestions for how to organise those papers.

In chapter 4, we'll move on to how to turn these records into accounts.

OK, what records *must* I keep?

Sole traders and partnerships, not registered for VAT

HMRC lay down the requirements for sole traders (**www.hmrc.gov.uk/sa/rec-keep-self-emp.htm**) and partnerships (**www.hmrc.gov.uk/sa/rec-keep-part-partners.htm**). They say that as a minimum, you must keep "a record of all your sales and takings and a record of all your purchases and expenses…so that you can fill in the tax return fully and accurately".

So at the very least, no matter how small your business is, you must keep records that'll let you fill in your self-assessment tax returns. We'll look at these returns in chapter 5. In the very simplest of cases this will just mean being able to add up your income and expenses for each year. HMRC don't lay down any specific rules for exactly how you must do this.

HMRC also say that your records can be either paper records or scanned on to a computer, except for certain records such as dividend vouchers for limited companies which HMRC say must be kept as paper records in their original form (**www.hmrc.gov.uk/ct/managing/record-keeping.htm#2**).

If you choose to scan in your records, the scanned documents must show all the information that was on the paper document, both on the front and the back, and they must be easily legible by HMRC. Don't save your files in an obscure format so that HMRC can't read them.

Registered for VAT

Even if your business is registered for VAT, there's still no set way to keep records, so follow the criteria above. That said, there are additional requirements that you must keep to when your business is registered for VAT. More on these shortly.

How should I produce an invoice?

Just about the only piece of paperwork that you'll have to create from scratch when it comes to the money side is an invoice to give to your customer each time you make a sale. If your business is registered for VAT, HMRC say that your invoice has to contain certain information.

Here's a sample VAT invoice.

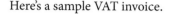
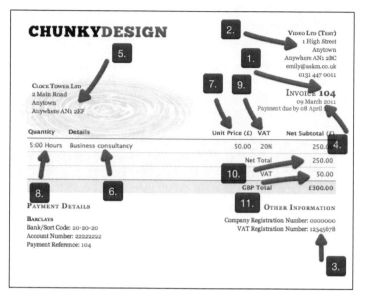

The numbered points show the information required by HMRC (**www.hmrc.gov.uk/vat/managing/charging/vat-invoices.htm**) on a VAT invoice:

1. Unique invoice number.
2. Your business's name and address. If your business is a limited company or LLP then you must show its registered address on its invoices.
3. Your business's VAT registration number. If your business is a limited company or LLP then its company/LLP registration number (supplied by Companies House) must also be included.
4. Invoice date.
5. Your customer's name and address.
6. A description to identify what you've supplied to the customer.
7. Unit price.

8. Quantity.

9. Rate of VAT on that item. (Exempt and zero-rated goods or services must show this on the invoice.)

10. Total amount payable by the customer, excluding VAT.

11. Total amount of VAT payable by the customer. Note that HMRC don't say you must include the grand total payable, but this is a good idea to avoid confusion and make sure the customer pays you what they should.

To help prompt payment you should also include your payment terms and methods, e.g. Payment due 30 days from invoice date by bank transfer to xx-xx-xx, a/c 12345678 or cheque made payable to MyCompanyName.

VAT-registered businesses must also keep a VAT account.

That means you need to be able to add up for each quarter what VAT you're due to pay to HMRC and what you can claim back, then take one away from the other to get what you're actually going to pay. If this sounds worrying, don't panic! Most accounting packages, both desktop and online, will do this for you. You can find out more about accounting packages in chapter 4.

Here's a sample invoice for a business that's not registered for VAT:

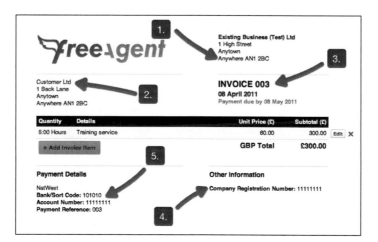

The numbered points are important to show on your invoices, even if your business is not registered for VAT:

1. Your business's name and address. If your business is a limited company or LLP then you must show its registered address on its invoices.

2. Your customer's name and address.

3. Unique invoice number, date and payment terms.

4. If your business is a limited company or LLP, its company/LLP registration number (supplied by Companies House).

5. Payment instructions, such as your bank account sort code and account number, or to whom cheques should be made payable. Customers who have to check how to pay, will take longer to pay!

If you're using an accounting software package to keep your records, these should automatically produce invoices that are fully compliant with HMRC's rules, be clearly laid out and match with your business's brand. I've used FreeAgent (**www.freeagent.com**) to create my sample invoices, but there are hundreds of alternative packages.

Even if you don't use a full-on accounting software package, you can use a package such as FreshBooks (**www.freshbooks.com**) to do your invoicing even though this is a Canadian package.

LLPs and Limited companies

Companies House don't have any requirements for *how* you must keep your financial records, just that you supply the necessary accounts to them every year.

HMRC don't require that limited companies keep their records in a specific format either. They explain that you need to keep records of your business's assets (what it owns), liabilities (what it owes), income and expenditure, and any stock you had at the end of your financial year. But you have to do that to prepare your accounts for Companies House anyway.

So you must make sure you have enough information so that you, or your accountant, can produce your business's accounts – which for these business types have to be in a set format, sometimes called "statutory accounts".

The other additional requirements about paperwork for LLPs and limited companies are to do with when the LLP or company must disclose its address and partners' or directors' details (**www.companieshouse.gov.uk/about/gbhtml/gp1.shtml#ch10**).

There are no additional requirements for invoices for limited companies, except that they must carry the company information as laid down by Companies House. See the above link.

So in brief, you must keep paperwork that enables you to prepare accounts for your business. These aren't just to keep HMRC happy at the end of the year. They also give you valuable information to help you run your business. We'll look more at this in chapter 4.

But for now let's move on to look at some of the actual paperwork you'll have to handle.

What paperwork will I have and how should I organise it?

You'll have a lot of different kinds of paperwork, such as:

- Invoices that you issue to your customers, to ask them to pay you for your goods or services, or receipts if payment is made upfront.

- Bills that your suppliers give you, which you need to pay.

- Bank statements.

- Receipts for payments that you don't have an invoice for, such as petrol, or milk bought from the corner shop, and small items that you pay for from the business's cash box.

- VAT returns, if your business is registered for VAT (see chapter 5).

- Other tax returns such as your self-assessment tax return.

- Information about any other money going in and out of the business, such as a lease agreement, or money you're paying back to an investor.

- Dividend vouchers, if your business is a limited company.

Don't be tempted to just bundle all this paperwork into a carrier bag and give it to your accountant once a year. For one thing, your accountant will almost inevitably get extremely fed up with this after a couple of years and end up giving you a quality of service that's much less than you and your business deserve. Your business is your baby so take good care of it and make sure you get the best service!

For another, this means you won't be able to get any sort of meaningful information about how your business is doing.

And last but not least, if HMRC ever come to call then you'll never be able to lay your hands on the vital piece of paper they're sure to want – and they can penalise businesses for poor record-keeping (**www.hmrc.gov.uk/about/new-penalties/new-penalties.pdf**).

Organise your paperwork carefully!

Raid your local stationer's for file dividers, plastic punch pockets and lever-arch files. Don't bother with ring-binders, you'll rapidly outgrow them.

Keep a file for each kind of record, for example, a file for invoices, a file for bills, a file for bank statements. Divide these files using your dividers. Some people like to file their paperwork alphabetically, others like to put it in date order, and some like to do both. Find a system that works for you, but just make sure you can quickly find any piece of paper. Yes, I do mean any one. You never know when you'll need to, for example, look up how much your accountant charged you on their last bill.

Separate out receipts for costs that you paid for personally, for example, using cash out of your own back pocket rather than cash out of your business's petty cash box (if it has one). It's important to keep these separate, especially if your business is a limited company. In that case, because you and your business are separate legal entities, the company can pay money you spend on most business expenses back to you, without attracting an extra tax charge.

Remember, make sure you keep all your pieces of paper, down to receipts from taxi drivers, and organise them so that you can find any one easily.

If you lose any of your pieces of paper, make a note of this, because HMRC say you must do your best to recreate your records if they're lost or destroyed. So make a note of what you bought when, and put a note in the "Additional Information" section of your tax return to let HMRC know that you've included estimated figures.

You may find, as your business goes on trading, that you have a lot of files to keep and you don't have room for them.

Consider investing in a scanner such as Doxie (**www.getdoxie.com**). This is a small scanner the size of a ruler, which works really well and doesn't produce gargantuan files like some scanners do. Scan all your papers (remember you have to scan them front and back to satisfy HMRC requirements) and keep the scanned documents.

> **Warning**
>
> Make sure you back up all your documents regularly; don't rely on keeping them on your computer, because computers can crash, break or be stolen. Use an external hard drive and/or an online backup service, such as Depositit (**www.depositit.com**), because if you shred them once they're scanned and then lose the scanned images, the documents are lost forever!

How long should I keep my paperwork for?

HMRC lay down rules for how long you should hang on to your paperwork after your tax return has been filed. If you're a sole trader or a partner in a partnership or LLP, you must keep your business's records for five years after the 31st January filing deadline for that tax year. So for the tax year ended 5th April 2013, the filing deadline is 31st January 2014, so you must keep your records for that year safely until 31st January 2019.

But if you file your tax return late, then you'll have to hang on to your records until either the usual date or fifteen months after you file your tax return, whichever is the later.

And if HMRC start a check into your tax return (**www.hmrc.gov.uk/sa/checks.htm**), you'll have to keep your records until HMRC write and tell you they've finished the check. HMRC undertake checks at random, so don't panic if your records are selected for checking – it doesn't mean they think you've done anything wrong. But if you file your tax return late they have longer to instigate a check – another incentive to file on time!

Limited companies must keep their records for at least six years from the end of their corporation tax accounting period, which is nearly always a year. There's more information about that in the next chapter. So if your company prepares its accounts to 31st March each year, you must store the company records for the year to 31st March 2013 until at least 31st March 2019.

I say "at least" because there are cases when HMRC say you must keep these records for longer (**www.hmrc.gov.uk/ct/managing/record-keeping.htm#2**). For example, if you buy a large piece of capital equipment (an *asset* – more on these in chapters 4 and 5), you must hang on to the invoice your supplier gave you when you bought the asset until six years after you sell or scrap the asset.

OK, so now you've organised your paperwork. But that's only the first part of the story.

You'll need to make sure you can turn the paperwork into accounts, whether these are just three figures on a tax return for a small sole trader, or a full set of accounts for a limited company.

Head on to chapter 4 and we'll look at that!

Chapter 4.

Simple accounts

Now that you've organised your paperwork, you're ready to start turning it into accounts!

For this, let's start at the end and work backwards. The end is what accounts you'll actually need. This depends on what your business structure is (see chapter 1) and why you're in business.

What accounts will I need?

If you're a sole trader, particularly if your business is a hobby business, then your accounts can be very simple indeed – essentially just a note of how much you've earned, less how much you've spent on day-to-day running expenses, to give your profit figure. (More about profit shortly.)

However, any expensive equipment that's going to last you for more than about a year needs to be treated differently. More about that in the next chapter. This is because if you're filling in a short tax return, which we'll also look at in the next chapter, you only need those figures – income, expenses, and equipment – for a year. We'll look at timespans at the end of the chapter.

Warning

Be careful. When you're adding up your income and expenses, you can't just add up how much money has come into your business bank account and gone out. When you look at adding up your income for the year, you have to include all the work you did during that year, no matter whether or not your customers paid you, or even if you've invoiced your customers for it yet. The upside of that, though, is that you can include any expenses you've incurred, not just those you've paid for.

But your records can do so much more than just help you fill in your tax return every year.

What extra information could my records give me?

There are two main areas this divides into: profit and cash.

Aren't they the same thing?

No, I'm afraid not!

Profit

Profit is your business's total income (also known as revenue) less all its day-to-day expenses that it has earned over a given period, which might be a month or a year. Your tax return nearly always shows profit or loss for a year. This information will be on what accountants call your business's "profit and loss account", or "P&L" for short.

Here's a very simple profit and loss account for a sole trader.

You can see that it covers a period of time, one year and also includes figures for last year so that the business owner can compare that with how his business did last year.

I've also included a margin figure at the bottom.

Jargon Buster

Your business's margin is its profit divided by its sales. It shows how much profit your business has made for every pound of sales it's earned.

This sole trader's margin has gone up, which is good news – it means he's making more profit for every pound of sales than he did last year.

J Hobson Writer and Photographer
Profit and Loss Account for the year ended 5th April 2011

		2011		2010
Income				
Writing		£6,000		£5,500
Photography		£7,500		£4,000
Total income		£13,500		£9,500
Expenses				
Travel	£2,000		£1,400	
Stationery	£1,850		£1,600	
Postage	£600		£500	
Entertaining	£450		£200	
Mileage	£2,000		£1,400	
Computer Software	£350		£350	
Accountancy	£400		£350	
Total expenses		£7,650		£5,800
Profit for the year		**£5,850**		**£3,700**
Margin		43%		39%

If your business is a limited company or LLP, the profit and loss account that it files at Companies House must be in a different, legally set format. Don't try and generate this yourself – leave it to your accountant.

Remember also that the income includes invoices that your customers haven't yet paid you for, and the day-to-day expenses includes costs that you haven't paid for yet.

These transactions won't affect your bank balance until the money actually comes in or goes out.

And there are also transactions that affect your cash but not your profit, such as when you buy a piece of equipment, because these don't count as day-to-day running costs.

The fact that there's cash in your business's bank account doesn't mean it's made a profit, and conversely your business can have made a profit but be overdrawn at the bank – and it's profit that your business pays tax on.

Why would I want to prepare a profit and loss account?

You may well want to know whether your business is making a profit, before you come to the point of filling in your tax return. You might not care if your hobby loses you money rather than earning it, but if you know what profit your business is making, you'll have some idea of how much tax you'll pay to HMRC on that profit.

Some profit questions to look at include:

Are your expenses outweighing your income?

Do you need to look for more customers, or put up your prices? Don't be afraid to charge what you're worth. Check out what your competitors are charging, and know how you're better than them. Are particular projects costing you more than others? Are you being too nice to certain clients?

Do you need to cut your costs?

For example, is your landlord charging you too much rent? Is there an alternative, such as cheaper office space, or working from home?

  ❝Why rent an office when your spare room, kitchen table or even your shed can do the job just as well – actually, even better? ❞ [8]

Is your bank charging you too much by way of charges? Do you need to change banks, or find more financing (see chapter 2) so that you don't go overdrawn or exceed agreed limits?

---

[8] Emma Jones, *Spare Room Start Up: How to Start a Business from Home*, Harriman House, 2008.

Could you reduce your costs by sourcing a cheaper supplier or using a free or lower-cost service, such as making phone calls through Skype (**www.skype.com**)?

> **Warning**
>
> If you do try and reduce costs in this way, do watch out for quality. The sound quality when you're making Skype calls to non-Skype phones can be poor.

Are you missing out on tax relief? The sole trader in the example hasn't put anything in for business use of his **❝ Think of your spend as a proportion of your £100 profit, not as a proportion of your £1,000 revenue. ❞** [9] home (see chapter 5 for more about how to work this out). That means he could be paying more tax than he needs to.

The simplified accounting method

This is also referred to as "cash accounting for small businesses", but I'm going to call it the "simplified accounting method" to avoid confusion with cash accounting for VAT. More about that in chapter 5.

You can start using the simplified accounting method if your annual sales, excluding any VAT, are under the VAT registration threshold, which is £79,000 as from 1st April 2013. You don't have to not be registered for VAT in order to use the simplified

---

[9] Liz Jackson and Mick Spain, *Start Up!*, ISBN 978-0-273-70602-1 (Pearson Education Ltd).

accounting method. Be careful, though, because this is annual sales overall. If you have more than one business, you have to add the sales from all of them together to check your eligibility. And you also have to use the method for all your businesses. You can't opt to use it for one but not another.

Once you've started using the simplified accounting method, you have to keep using that method until your annual sales go over £158,000, unless you have a genuine business reason to stop using it.

The simplified accounting method just means that instead of including income in your business's books when you have invoiced your customers for it, you include it when they have paid you.

Also, costs are included when you paid for them, not when you incurred them.

And if you're using the simplified accounting method you would include large pieces of equipment as part of your day-to-day running costs, rather than having to calculate depreciation. We'll look more at large pieces of equipment shortly.

Simplified expenses

Businesses that are eligible to use the simplified accounting method, whether or not they are actually using it, also have the option to account for three kinds of costs in a simpler way than adding up the actual cost.

The first is business use of home, which we'll look at more in the next chapter.

The second is to include motor expenses using the mileage method. We'll look more closely at this in the next chapter.

The third is if you are living at your business premises, for example if you are running a bed and breakfast from your home. In that case, instead of having to work out the proportion of how much you use the property for business and how much for personal, you can add up all your property costs and then deduct a fixed allowance for personal use.

There is more information about the simplified accounting method and expense calculations from HMRC (**www.hm-treasury.gov.uk/d/simpler_income_tax_for_simplest_small_bu siness_mar2013.pdf**).

Cash

You need to also have a handle on your business's cashflow, so that you know if your business is in danger of running out of cash. You can tell if your business could run short by looking at what accountants call its "balance sheet". That just means a summary of what your business owns (its assets), less what it owes (its liabilities), at any point in time. If your business owes more than it owns, you're in trouble.

The following shows a very simple balance sheet for a sole trader who is not using the simplified accounting method.

Jargon Buster

Fixed Assets = large items of equipment owned by the business. This sole trader is a writer and photographer, so included in here would be his cameras and his computer to enhance and edit pictures. These go in at their initial cost and then their value is spread over their useful life using an adjustment called "depreciation".

Current Assets = assets the business owns that can easily be converted into hard cash, for example, stock of the product(s) that your business sells.

Debtors = money owed to your business, such as invoices that your customers haven't yet paid you for.

Creditors = money your business owes, such as to its suppliers, its staff, and to HMRC for VAT.

Net current assets = current assets less any creditors falling due within 1 year, which are also called Current Liabilities.

Net assets = all assets less all liabilities. This would be Net Liabilities if it were a negative figure. If this figure is negative then your business is in trouble because if all its creditors asked to be repaid at once, this wouldn't be possible.

Capital Account = money you put into, and took out of the business.

J Hobson Writer and Photographer Balance Sheet as at 5th April 2011					
		2011			2010
Fixed Assets		£3,000			£4,000
Current Assets					
Debtors	£3,600			£2,000	
Cash at bank and in hand	£1,200			£1,000	
	£4,800			£3,000	
Creditors: amounts falling due within 1 year		-£2,000			-£1,400
Net current assets		£2,800			£1,600
Net assets		**£5,800**			**£5,600**
Capital account		**£5,800**			**£5,600**

This is a healthy-looking business, because its balance sheet total figure ("Net assets") is positive. It has enough cash and other assets available to pay all its debts straight away, if needed.

If your business is a limited company or LLP, the balance sheet that it files at Companies House will not look very different from this, but it will have a legal disclosure at the bottom for you to sign as director.

Your balance sheet total, or net assets, might be less than it could be. Here's why:

Is enough money coming into your business?

Do you need to tighten your credit control? This might include getting your customers to pay you more quickly, jettisoning customers who are slow- or non-payers, and taking payment by credit card or PayPal.

Do you have too few customers?

It can be dangerous for a small business to depend on a few large customers, or even worse, one large customer, because they can use their purchasing power to pay you very late or, in the worst case scenario, not at all. And if you lose their custom, your business could be in serious trouble.

Can you afford to give your customers credit at all?

Consider asking for full payment upfront, or a deposit before you start working on the project. But if you do, make sure you offer a full refund if customers aren't happy, otherwise you'll end up like the budget airlines, with a lot of bad publicity.

Think carefully about at what point in the buying process you ask your customers to pay.

True story

My husband and I went to a hotel in Penrith for Sunday lunch. Usually you'd pay for a meal either after you've finished if you're served at your table, or when you collect your food if you're eating in a café with counter service, right?

This hotel served us at our table, but brought over a credit card machine and asked us to pay when they served us our food – so we had to go through the chip and PIN rigmarole while our food was sitting there getting cold.

We've never been back there since!

Consider fixing all your prices, even if you're in an industry which traditionally charges by the hour. That way your customers know in advance what they'll have to pay you, and you'll have a much clearer idea of how much income you are generating. See chapter 7 for more about planning your income for the future.

What costs do you have to meet?

What costs will your business incur? For example, if you take on a large new contract, will this need you to spend money upfront?

Let's take an example. Susan makes soft furnishings. She wins a new contract to make cushions and curtains for her local hotel, which is being refurbished. She will have to buy materials and trimmings for these and usually this would be before the hotel pays her. She needs to consider taking a deposit so that she has some cash to put towards the fabric.

What taxes will you have to pay, and when? See chapter 5 for more information about this.

Do you have enough money set aside to pay your suppliers?

Remember how quickly you need to pay your suppliers. Quick payment encourages good relations with your suppliers, but could put a brake on your business's cashflow. Your suppliers' invoices should show their credit terms, e.g. payment due within 14 days of receipt of invoice, or 30 days from receipt of goods, or payment due by return, i.e. as soon as the invoice arrives.

So there is a wealth of information that your business's records can give you!

This could lead to you wanting to add up the numbers more than the once a year that's required for tax purposes. We'll look at this right at the end of this chapter.

Some businesses crunch their numbers once a month so that they can review their profit and loss account and balance sheet. These are called "management accounts" because you use them to manage and run your business.

What if I don't want to do management accounts?

You still need to be able to keep track of every transaction in your business, from all the invoices you've issued to your customers, to money that you spent on a taxi to go and visit a client. This is because those transactions have all got to be included when you work out the figures to go on your tax return. The more transactions your business has, the more complicated your accounting will get, especially if you handle a lot of cash (for example, you run a shop, or you're a tradesman who's often paid in cash by his customers).

You'll also need to break your expenses down by category, for example you'll need to keep a list of travel expenses, a list of stationery expenses, and so on. It's a good idea to do this as you go, because it's much easier to remember what you spent yesterday than what you spent last month, or even, heaven forbid, last year.

Even if you're a sole trader filling in a short tax return (see chapter 5), this is important, because HMRC can inspect any business's records, and may say that your records aren't being kept properly if they can't see a breakdown of expenses – and remember that they can fine you for this (**www.hmrc.gov.uk/about/new-penalties/new-penalties.pdf**).

Do I have to produce more complicated accounts each year than just a list of invoices and a list of expenses?

If your business is of any other type than a sole trader, it needs to produce more in-depth accounts because partnerships and LLPs need to share their profit between more than one person, and for LLPs and limited companies there's a legally set format that accounts have to be in when they go to Companies House.

Companies House say that limited companies and LLPs *must* keep a track of what they own (assets) and what they owe (liabilities) as well as income and expenses. But, as we've seen above, it's a good idea to keep a handle on what your business owns and owes in any case.

This all sounds a bit scary. Are there tools that can help me?

Yes! The tools you'd choose from would be a handwritten cashbook, a spreadsheet, a desktop-based accounting package, or an online accounting package.

Let's look further at each of these.

Handwritten cashbook

This works well if:

- Your business is tiny and has only a few transactions going in and out. This will be true for some hobby businesses, but also for some freelance businesses such as IT contractors, who might only have one or two customers and very few costs.

- You're handy with a calculator.

- You really can't face using a computer at all.

But using a handwritten cashbook does have its drawbacks:

- A cashbook is time-consuming to write up.

- Cashbooks are error-prone (it's easy to add up a string of numbers wrongly when you're using a calculator). But many accountants prefer a neat set of paper records to a messy set of computer records (I certainly do).

- You have to work everything out, including the correct VAT, which can be very difficult.

- You'll be without your books for weeks if not months every year, while your accountant prepares your tax return.

- A cashbook can't give you an instant profit and loss account and balance sheet to provide helpful information to help you run your business.

- If you're using a cashbook, your accountant can only ever act as a bean-counter rather than a trusted adviser, because he/she won't have enough information about your business to be anything else.

The other options all involve using a computer in some way, so if you haven't got a computer, you'll need to either buy one, or use a cashbook.

Computerised records

Warning

Don't fall into the trap of assuming if it's on the computer, it's right. The first rule of using a computer package to do your accounts is garbage in, garbage out!

The first option for keeping your accounting records on the computer is a basic spreadsheet.

Spreadsheet

Spreadsheets work well if:

- You're used to using them. Don't try learning spreadsheets for the first time to do your business bookkeeping – it's too important.

- You're good at spotting errors in a spreadsheet.

- Your business doesn't have too many transactions.

- You're happy to create formulae to set up your own profit and loss and balance sheets on the spreadsheet.

Their drawbacks are:

- Creating and maintaining a spreadsheet can be time-consuming.

- When it comes to passing information to your accountant, it can be difficult to track who's got the latest version of the spreadsheet. If you send a copy to your accountant, she makes some changes, and you make some changes while it's with her, on your version... chaos!

- Spreadsheets are error-prone. Miss one line of an @sum formula and your VAT and tax figures will be wrong, which could land you in hot water with HMRC.

- You have to remember to update your spreadsheets, for example if the VAT rate changes, and ensure the new rate only applies to invoices on or after that date.

- It can be difficult for your accountant to turn spreadsheets into meaningful information if your business has more than a few small transactions.

- It's difficult to create a profit and loss account and balance sheet from a spreadsheet, unless you're comfortable with how to create them. Believe me, I've tried!

- All this means that your accountant will be a bean-counter rather than a trusted adviser.

If you want to set up a series of basic spreadsheets for your business bookkeeping, check out James Smith's book.[10]

Using a cashbook or spreadsheet is just too much hassle. Isn't there software that does all that for me?

Yes there is. There are two types of software – desktop packages and online applications.

---

[10] James Smith BSc ACA, *Keeping it Simple: Small Business Bookkeeping, Cash Flow, Tax and VAT*, ISBN 978-1-907302-16-9 (Taxcafe UK Ltd).

Desktop accounting software

Why "desktop"? Because you download the software, or load it from a CD, on to a computer.

The most widely used desktop accounting software packages are Sage 50 (**www.sage.co.uk**) and QuickBooks (**www.intuit.co.uk/quickbooks**).
When do these packages work well?

They're good if:

• You have quite a large business. For smaller, simpler businesses they can be too complicated and you end up trying to use a sledgehammer to crack a walnut.

• You're used to using them. If you want to use one of these packages, certainly Sage 50, and you don't know double-entry bookkeeping, get yourself some training. Sage 50 in particular is a complex package and is written in accounting-speak rather than plain English.

• You're in a rural area with no, or slow, broadband connection, so using an online system wouldn't work for you.

• You'd like to have a profit and loss account and balance sheet produced for you automatically as you enter your transactions.

But they come with disadvantages too:

• Just like using a spreadsheet, swapping backups with your accountant can cause problems as to who's got the latest version of your books, because someone has to remember not to make any changes.

• Support often costs extra for these packages. Like a budget airline, a low upfront cost can be misleading.

• Upgrades (for VAT rate changes, etc.) often cost extra too.

• Your security is in their hands (although online software companies do guard heavily against risk).

Online accounting software

As well as desktop-based software, there are a growing number of online software packages, which you access through your web browser over the Internet so you don't need to download or install anything.

Some of the most popular packages available in the UK are FreeAgent (**www.freeagent.com**), Xero (**www.xero.com**) and KashFlow (**www.kashflow.co.uk**).

These packages work really well if:

- You're happy working online.

- You don't understand double-entry bookkeeping. These packages are often very easy to use and written in plain English, not in accounting-speak.

- You're on the move a lot. Online accounting software can be accessed anywhere and from any computer, so long as you have Internet access.

- You have a good broadband connection.

- You're concerned about how secure your data would be Security is a high priority for companies like these three, and accounts kept on a desktop accounting package are only as secure as the computer they're on.

- You think you might forget to take regular backups. Online accounting packages have automatic backup and disaster recovery routines built in so that your data isn't lost. They also have policies in place to allow you to export your data if the company goes wheels up.

- You're happy to share data online with your accountant. You can give your accountant access to view your figures without needing to send them anything. This makes it much easier to communicate with your accountant and lets them be a trusted adviser rather than a bean-counter.

- You want daily up-to-date business information. Online accounting software is often best for this because you can upload bank statements directly into it.

- You'd like to have a profit and loss account and balance sheet produced for you automatically as you enter your transactions.

- You want a product tailored for small business. Online software is often more modern, recently developed because online is very much the future of accounting software – and online packages will often have been built by people who saw a gap in the market for an application to keep their own small business books. That's certainly true of FreeAgent.[11]

The only disadvantage I can see to keeping your books online is that you can't do this if you don't have internet access, for example if you live in a rural area that has poor broadband connectivity. If you try and keep your books online using a dial-up connection you'll very quickly get so frustrated that you'll want to hurl your computer out of the window!

Do I need to learn double-entry bookkeeping to keep my records?

No. You didn't go into business to be an accountant!

Put it this way, it took me months to fully get to grips with double-entry bookkeeping. So I'm not going to inflict that on you in this book. I'm going to save the space for explaining what expenses you can claim tax relief on, and useful things like that. If you use either desktop or online accounting software, that will do the double-entry for you anyway.

---

[11] Well I would say that – I work there! But I promise I'm not getting paid by them to write this book.

Isn't it easier just to hire a bookkeeper?

You could do.

There are a lot of self-employed bookkeepers who will use a software package to keep your records for you. You can either find a bookkeeper by asking for recommendations from your business contacts, or through the Institute of Certified Bookkeepers (**www.bookkeepers.org.uk**). Alternatively, try looking on sites such as PeoplePerHour (**www.peopleperhour.com**) or Elance (**www.elance.com**), where freelance bookkeepers advertise.

If your business has a lot of transactions (for instance, you run a retail shop and don't have an EPOS system), and you're very busy in your business, then you could do well to hire a bookkeeper.

But if your business doesn't have a large number of transactions, and you're happy using software, it's perfectly possible to keep your books yourself.

✱✱✱

Hopefully that's helped you decide how much financial information you'd like to have about your business, and what system you might use to turn your paperwork into that information.

Before we go into tax in more depth, I'd just like to look at which date you should prepare your accounts to each year.

Why for a year?

Because the tax on your business's profits, which is corporation tax for a limited company and income tax for any other business type, is payable on profit for a year at a time. So you need to prepare accounts for your business for a full year even if you don't do monthly management accounts.

The date to which you prepare your business's accounts is called its "accounting year end" or "year end" for short.

Which year end should I choose for my business?

Sole trader / partnership / LLP

If your business is a sole trader, partnership or LLP, the easiest year end to choose is either 31st March or 5th April. This is because the UK's tax year, or "fiscal year", ends on 5th April each year and it's much easier to fill in your tax returns when your year end coincides with this.

You'll also be able to save time by filling in the short self-employed pages of your tax return if you're a sole trader with a year end that matches the fiscal year, which you almost certainly can't if you have any other year end. More information about that in chapter 5.

(HMRC say that you can prepare accounts to 31st March each year and treat them as if they matched the fiscal year.)

It's perfectly OK to choose any other date you like or that suits your business in terms of cashflow. For instance, if you prepare your accounts to 30th April each year then you'll actually pay tax on those profits a year later than you would if you'd prepared the accounts to 31st March. This is because the figures you put on your tax return, and pay tax on, are from the accounts whose year end fell in that fiscal year. (Special rules apply for the years when your business starts and stops.)

So when we look at the fiscal year that ended on 5th April 2013, a set of accounts for the year to 31st March 2013 finishes in that fiscal year – but so does a set of accounts for the year to 30th April 2012.

But using a year end other than one that matches the fiscal year can cause awful muddles, particularly when your business starts and stops. Even tax lecturers recommend using 31st March or 5th April, and what's good enough for them is good enough for me!

Income tax is payable at the same times each year for all these businesses, no matter when its year end is. More about that in chapter 5.

Limited companies

For a limited company, corporation tax is payable 9 months and 1 day after that company's year end, rather than at the same time each calendar year.

Tax rates for limited companies are set to 31st March each year. The year to 31st March for limited companies is called the "financial year".

If your business is a limited company, you don't have to prepare accounts to match the financial year, but it's easier to do that. This is because, as the director of a limited company, you have to fill in an annual self-assessment tax return and you have to include your salary and dividend income from the company – for the fiscal year to 5th April. So it's much easier to get that information if your company's accounts run to 31st March each year.

But do watch your cashflow when you choose your year end, particularly if your company is registered for VAT. As we'll see in the next chapter, VAT is usually payable four times a year and it might cause your business problems if its corporation tax bill and VAT bill fall due at the same time.

When you first register your limited company, Companies House automatically make its first year end a year from the end of the month in which it was incorporated. For example, my own limited company, Home Business Accountant Ltd, was formed in mid-February 2007, so Companies House gave it a first year end of 29th February 2008. I filed a form to change that to 31st March 2008.[12] It's perfectly OK to prepare your company's first set of accounts for more than a year, but they mustn't go over 18 months.

---

[12] And Companies House still made me do the form again because I'd put 28th February instead of 29th February by mistake. For Pete's sake!

Limited companies can nearly always only change their year end once every 5 years.

My business's accounts are used to fill in the tax return. Does anyone else need to see them?

Yes. Limited companies and LLPs must file accounts every year with Companies House, within 9 months of the year end, or risk a fine – and the fines stack up the longer the accounts are delayed (**www.companieshouse.gov.uk/companiesAct/ca_lateFilingPen alties.shtml**).

Any business might also need to show accounts to a bank manager, or other lender.

Case study

Your name: John O'Nolan

Your business's name: John O'Nolan (Sole Trader)

Your business's website: john.onolan.org

What does your business do?

I'm a freelance interactive designer. Which is to say that I design user interfaces – primarily for website and mobile applications. I work both as a contractor to major corporations such as Virgin Atlantic and Microsoft, as well as on my own projects and ventures.

How did you come to start your business?

I started out, as most do, by working full time for a web design agency. Running my own business was what I'd wanted to do since I was about 16 years old. After a couple of years I decided that I'd learned a sufficient amount about the industry and I was ready to take on the challenge of working for myself.

Luckily, starting a web design business doesn't require much, if any, investment. I already owned all the equipment that I needed to do the job so it was really just a case of sitting down, finding clients and getting the work done.

What difficulties did you face with your business's finances?

My biggest mistake in the beginning was, I'm sorry to say, acting upon the advice of an accounting company. It was probably my own mistake for not researching a suitable accountant for my business, but they recommended that I set myself up as a limited company and register for VAT. They explained all the tax benefits and why it would be suited to me. And who was I to argue? They're the experts. A good accountant will make your business money, I was told.

While I'm sure a limited company structure and (non-mandatory) VAT registration is beneficial for many businesses, for mine it was a disaster. The sheer amount of administration required to complete my accounts properly wasn't only time-consuming and un-profitable, it was also downright depressing.

Why did these difficulties occur? For example, did you try to manage the books yourself?

Being a one-man company, I absolutely have to do my own bookkeeping. Not just because it would be too expensive to outsource it, but because I need to stay in touch with the finances of my business. I need to know exactly how much I'm making, how much I'm spending, and everything in between. Unfortunately my accounting company's method of *send us all your invoices and expenses each month* meant that I was resigned to a lowly, half-baked spreadsheet that told me... well not much of anything at all really.

It left me, quite literally, with my head in my hands every time I had to even think about anything to do with my accounts. I had no idea what to do with any of it.

How did you remedy this? For example, did you get an accountant, sack your accountant, use software, or go on a bookkeeping course?

About three months into business, a friend of mine told me about an online accounting application called FreeAgent. I'd heard of similar US-based services before, but this was the first really modern accounting web application that I'd come across which was suited to the UK market. FreeAgent would let me import my bank statements and reconcile them against my invoices and expenses. Then it would create graphs of all my account balances and automatically generate cashflow reports and even my tax returns.

I told my accountants about this great new service, and how it allowed me to keep track of my bookkeeping and give them access to it instantly online, rather than posting them paper invoices and receipts every month and leaving me in the dark. Instead of being greeted by warm-hearted enthusiasm and a willingness to help their client, they told me that they were unable to support FreeAgent-based accounting. They didn't say why, other than that they didn't like it. Whether or not it was good for me and my business didn't seem to factor into the equation.

I fired them immediately.

Using FreeAgent by myself, I was more efficient and had a better understanding of my accounts than at any point when I'd had an expensive accounting agency doing the work for me. Eventually I transitioned to being a sole trader and I now have a (FreeAgent friendly) accountant check over my books and complete my tax returns for me periodically. This has suited me much better than my previous setup.

The real icing on the cake, of course, is that I don't pay for FreeAgent. They actually pay me to use it now. As if the software wasn't already worth three times the monthly premium, FreeAgent also have a referral program which discounts your monthly premium (permanently) by 10% every time you refer a new customer. Refer 10 customers and you use the software free of charge. Refer more than 10 customers and they give you a percentage of the fees from all the people you've referred, every single month.

It's sort of like buying your favourite cake in the whole world. Then being told you can have that cake for free whenever you want. Then being told that each month you're going to be sent free cake, and an envelope full of cash to go along with it. I don't really know how else to put it. You'd have to be fairly crazy not to want to use FreeAgent.

As a result do you think that finance and accounts can be dealt with in-house?

I absolutely think that accounts can be dealt with in-house. I still think it's advisable (and prudent) to have your accounts audited by a professional once in a while. But day-to-day bookkeeping can, in my experience, be done in-house with ease. I reconcile all my accounts once a month; it generally takes me 5 minutes and involves no stress at all.

***

Phew, that chapter was a bit of a mouthful!

Go and grab a cup of coffee, and/or a large glass of wine, and/or a gooey pastry, to fortify yourself to look at tax in the next chapter!

Chapter 5.

Tax

"In this world nothing can be said to be certain, except death and taxes."[13]

That's quite right!

When you're in business, no matter how small your business is, you need to think about tax on some level or another. In this chapter, we'll have a look at some of the most common taxes that businesses need to consider. We'll start with VAT, then move on to taxes that are paid on a business's profit – income tax, National Insurance, and corporation tax.

VAT

VAT stands for Value Added Tax, or, as my husband calls it, Very Awkward Tax, because it's full of little anomalies.

It's a tax that some businesses have to pay on their sales. I say some because your business only has to pay VAT if it's registered with HMRC for VAT.

And even for VAT-registered businesses, not all sales are actually subject to VAT. For example, if your business sells insurance, insurance is exempt from VAT and therefore isn't a VATable sale.

---

[13] Benjamin Franklin, 1789.

If your business is registered for VAT, you have to charge VAT on all your VATable sales. This is called "output tax" or "output VAT".

You'll also be entitled to claim back some – but not all – of the VAT that you pay to your suppliers. That's called "input tax" or "input VAT".

More about output VAT and input VAT later in this chapter.

Do all businesses have to register for VAT if they're making VATable sales?

No.

You don't have to register if your business's total VATable sales for the year – on a rolling basis so you do need to check this each month – are under the limit set by HMRC. From 1st April 2013 that limit is £79,000, and HMRC usually increase it every year.

You also have to register if your sales are going to go over the limit in the next 30 days.

Should I register my business anyway, even if I don't have to?

That depends largely on who your customers are, and how much you spend on costs that have VAT on them – which is most costs.

If you sell mostly to larger businesses, they will almost certainly be VAT-registered, and be able to reclaim the VAT on the invoices you give them.

But if your customers are smaller businesses, they might not be VAT-registered, so if you register, that would mean your bills are effectively higher, possibly when compared to your competitors'.

And if your customers are the general public, they definitely won't be VAT-registered, because only businesses can register for VAT.

How does it work that your bills are effectively higher for non-VAT registered customers, if your business is registered?

Let's take an example. Jack is a painter and decorator. He charges £20 per hour. His customers are householders, so they definitely won't be VAT-registered. If Jack were to register for VAT, he would have to charge his customers £20 + VAT per hour – so £24 per hour.

Alternatively, he could keep his price at £20, but then it would have to include VAT, so Jack would only get to keep £16.67 per hour. The rest would be the VAT that he would have to pay to HMRC.

Assuming Jack does increase his price, his customers can't reclaim the extra £4 from HMRC, so that means Jack's services have just got 20% more expensive for them. If Jack's customers were other VAT-registered businesses, they could reclaim the £4 as input VAT from HMRC so there's no extra cost to them.

How do I register my business for VAT?

It's best done online through HMRC's website (**online.hmrc.gov.uk/registration/newbusiness/introduction**).

You can also apply to file your VAT returns online at the same time. (**search2.hmrc.gov.uk/kb5/hmrc/forms/view.page?formid=986 &record=OmPa6ruQM2U**).

If you have any queries about VAT then you can ring HMRC's National Advice Service on 0845 010 9000.

What other advantages and disadvantages are there to registering for VAT?

Some people think that registering for VAT gives extra kudos and make your business seem more like a "real" one.

But there are disadvantages:

- Being registered for VAT does entail extra paperwork. You have to complete a quarterly VAT return and submit it to HMRC. See below for more about that.

- Your invoices must be in a set format if your business is registered for VAT. See chapter 4 for more information about this.

- HMRC also have the right to inspect your books to make sure you're doing everything right for VAT. This can be disruptive for your business.

- And in essence, if you register for VAT you're acting as an unpaid tax collector for HMRC!

Unpaid tax collector? How does that work?

Let's go back a few steps.

I mentioned earlier in this chapter about output and input VAT. If your business is registered for VAT, you must charge your customers output VAT on all your VATable sales. This will usually be at the standard rate (20% at the time of writing), but might also be at the reduced rate (5%), or even at zero rate (0%).

If you're making zero-rated sales, such as hiring out minibuses with drivers, you are still technically charging your customers output VAT. It's just that the rate of VAT will be 0%. 5% VAT applies mainly to domestic costs such as electricity and gas used in the home.

There are also some sales which are exempt from VAT (such as insurance) and outside the scope of VAT (such as MOT tests). These two categories are both non-VATable sales.

Let's crunch some numbers.

Rob is a self-employed management consultant. His business is registered for VAT.

He charges one of his customers £5,000. He has to add output VAT of 20% to that, because management consultancy is chargeable to VAT at the standard rate.

So the total amount that Rob's customer will pay him for that invoice will be £6,000.

The extra £1,000 is Rob's output VAT which he must record on his VAT return and pay to HMRC.

But Rob is unlikely to have to pay the full £1,000, because he can deduct from that any input VAT he's paid to his suppliers.

Rob bought a computer which cost him £300 + VAT, so a total of £360.

The £60 is input VAT which he can reclaim from HMRC.

Be careful, though, as not all the VAT you pay to your suppliers can be reclaimed as input VAT. For example, entertaining anyone except your business's employees will have VAT on it – but HMRC say you can't claim that VAT back.

HMRC also say you can't reclaim input VAT if your supplier didn't give you a proper VAT invoice.

If you're in doubt, check with your accountant or with a VAT expert (**www.vatark.co.uk**). You can also ring HMRC's VAT helpline on 0845 010 9000.

Each quarter, Rob will add up the output VAT that he's charged to his customers, then take off the input VAT that he can reclaim. He'll do this in a different way depending on how he is accounting for VAT. More about that in a moment.

The result of that calculation will be what he'll pay to HMRC – or receive back from HMRC, if his total input VAT is more than his total output VAT.

He will give these figures to HMRC on his VAT return.

In this case, Rob has charged £1,000 in output VAT and can reclaim £60 in input VAT, so he will pay £940 to HMRC.

Here's what Rob's VAT return will look like.

```
VAT Return for the period 2011-06 (not yet filed)
```

Dates:		Calculation Basis:	Invoice
2011-04-01 - 2011-06-30		Fuel Scale Charge:	None
Flat Rate Scheme:		Electronic Return Due:	2011-08-07
Not on Flat Rate Scheme		Electronic Payment Due:	2011-08-07

VAT due on sales and other outputs	**1**	£1,000.00
VAT due on acquisitions from other EC Member States	**2**	£0.00
Total VAT due (the sum of boxes 1 and 2)	**3**	£1,000.00
VAT reclaimed on purchases and other inputs (including acquisitions from the EC)	**4**	£60.00
Net VAT to be paid to Customs or reclaimed by you (Difference between boxes 3 and 4)	**5**	£940.00
Total value of sales and all other outputs excluding any VAT.	**6**	£5,300
Total value of purchases and all other inputs excluding any VAT.	**7**	£300
Total value of all supplies of goods and related costs, excluding any VAT, to other EC member states.	**8**	£0
Total value of acquisitions of goods and related costs excluding any VAT, from other EC member states.	**9**	£0

How often does a registered business have to file a VAT return with HMRC?

It's standard practice to do a VAT return four times a year.

There is an annual scheme which lets you only make a return once a year, but I've only ever known one business use it, and to be honest, that proved more trouble than it was worth. You still have to work out how much you should have paid for the whole year, and you still have to pay VAT over to HMRC every quarter, so I'd stick with quarterly.

You can choose whether you'll choose to file returns for the quarters ended:

- March, June, September and December – this is the most common and accountants call it "calendar quarters" because it matches with the calendar year,

- February, May, August and November, or

- January, April, July and October.

It'll make your accountant's life easier if you make your VAT quarters coincide with your business's accounting year end. So if your business's year end is 28th February, pick the second set of quarters.

You have to file your business's VAT return within a calendar month of the end of the quarter. Be careful though, and watch your cashflow. You have to pay VAT at the same time as the VAT return is filed (though you get an extra 7 days to file and pay if you do both online). In the above example, because Rob's VAT return is for the quarter ended 30th June, he'll have to pay his VAT by 7th August.

But he'll have had income tax and National Insurance to pay by 31st July (more about that later in this chapter where we look at tax on profits) – so he has two big tax bills following on quickly one after the other.

That could be bad news for his business's supply of cash!

VAT returns must now almost inevitably be filed online with HMRC (**www.hmrc.gov.uk/vat/vat-online/submit.htm**).

You can also register to have HMRC automatically take payment of VAT from your business's bank account by direct debit. This saves you having to remember to pay your VAT, and you get a bit longer to pay too – an extra 5 days on top of the 7 extra days you get for paying online, so an extra 12 days altogether.

Different ways of accounting for VAT

There are several different ways in which Rob could do his sums for VAT.

If he's using what HMRC call the "standard accounting scheme", and what accountants often call "invoice accounting", he'll add up his output and input VAT based on the invoices he's issued to his customers and the bills he's received from his suppliers – regardless of whether his customers have actually paid him and whether he's actually paid his suppliers. This is based on when the invoices and bills are dated, not when they were issued.

For example, if today's date is 5th April, and Rob issues an invoice with a date of 20th March, then assuming he is invoice accounting, this invoice must go into his quarter that ends on 31st March – not 30th June.

For some businesses, this is a good scheme to use. If your customers always pay you on the nail (for example, retail businesses), and you take time to pay your suppliers, then invoice accounting will be good for your cashflow.

But for many businesses it can cause problems, because most customers don't always pay immediately.

HMRC do offer an alternative, which is called the "cash accounting scheme" (**www.hmrc.gov.uk/vat/start/schemes/cash.htm**).

If you're cash accounting, then you only pay output VAT to HMRC once your customers have actually paid you. You'd also only be able to reclaim input VAT once you've actually paid your suppliers.

You don't have to apply to HMRC to join the cash accounting scheme, but not all businesses can use it. Your estimated annual VATable sales for the next 12 months must be under a certain limit (£1.35 million at the moment) for your business to be eligible to join the scheme.

There are also other prohibitions such as not having committed a VAT offence in the last 12 months (**www.hmrc.gov.uk/vat/start/schemes/cash.htm**).

Flat rate scheme

There's also another scheme called the "flat rate scheme" (**www.hmrc.gov.uk/vat/start/schemes/flat-rate.htm**), which is only applicable to small businesses, that is businesses making VATable sales less than £150,000 a year (before VAT).

Under the flat rate scheme, you still have to produce VAT invoices and charge output VAT to your customers as normal. But, each quarter, instead of adding up the output VAT you've actually charged to your customers and then deducting the input VAT you've paid your suppliers, you work out the amount you pay to HMRC differently.

You add up your total sales including the output VAT you've charged, and then multiply that figure by a certain percentage, depending on what your business does. For example, as a management consultant, Rob's percentage would be 14%.

The percentages are laid down by HMRC and they're worked out to allow for the amount of input VAT your business would usually pay if it weren't using the flat rate scheme (**www.hmrc.gov.uk/vat/start/schemes/flat-rate.htm**).

Because of this, you can't claim any input VAT when you're on the flat rate scheme, unless you buy a large asset costing £2,000 or more including VAT. So instead of paying £940, if he were using the flat rate scheme, Rob would pay £6,000 x 14% = £840, and save £100 that quarter.

Here's what Rob's VAT return would look like if he were using the flat rate scheme.

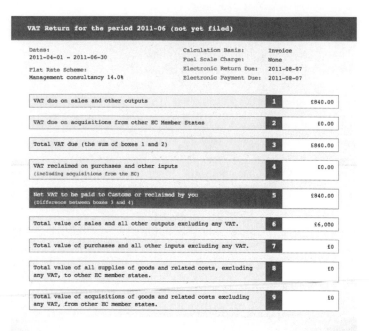

It's the same form that Rob fills in, but the figures are different. In particular, box 6, although it says that it includes sales net of VAT, actually includes sales inclusive of VAT. That is correct when your business is on the VAT flat rate scheme.

Can using the flat rate scheme save my business money?

It's not intended for that. HMRC designed it to save small businesses time in bookkeeping (and I don't think it actually does that, because you will still have to add up all your figures anyway when you do your accounts). But in some cases, like Rob's, using the VAT flat rate scheme can save your business cash, particularly if your business's main cost is your own labour.

I know of one case where freelance social workers, whose flat rate is 10%, were able to make significant savings because the flat rate percentage for social work is comparatively low, and they wouldn't have been able to reclaim much input VAT if they hadn't used the VAT flat rate scheme.

Be careful, though. When you add up the sales you make on the flat rate scheme in order to work out your VAT, you must also include other income that you probably wouldn't think should be included, such as exempt sales (**www.hmrc.gov.uk/vat/start/schemes/flat-rate.htm**).

So using the flat rate scheme can potentially cost your business money rather than saving it.

Make sure you crunch your numbers!

Can I start using the flat rate scheme straight away?

You do need to apply to HMRC to join the flat rate scheme. This can't be done online yet, so you need to use a paper form, which you can download from HMRC's website (**search2.hmrc.gov.uk/kb5/hmrc/forms/view.page?formid=102 7&record=awaDOY_u094**).

I want to use the cash accounting scheme. Can I also use the flat rate scheme?

The flat rate scheme has its own cash-based accounting method which works just like the cash accounting scheme. So when you're on the flat rate scheme, and you're doing your VAT calculation, you can either add up all the sales you've invoiced your customers for or you can use the cash-based accounting method and add up all the receipts that came in from your customers.

***

That was a quick introduction to VAT. Now let's look at taxes your business pays on its profits, rather than its sales.

Tax on your business's profit: income tax, National Insurance and corporation tax

For sole traders, partnerships and LLPs, you, personally, will pay income tax and National Insurance on your share of your business's profit. For sole traders, that is, of course, 100%.

As we saw in chapter 4, the UK's tax year, or fiscal year, runs from 6th April one year to 5th April the following year.

Useless but interesting fact

Why does the fiscal year end on such a funny date?

In bygone times, the new year didn't start on 1st January. It started on 25th March, which is Lady Day in the church calendar. When Britain adopted the Gregorian calendar in 1752, to catch up with the rest of Europe eleven days had to be cut out of the British calendar, so the new tax year began on 6th April instead of 25th March.

The tax year is given a number each year, based on the two calendar years it partly covers. So, for example, the tax year that started on 6th April 2013 and finishes on 5th April 2014 is called 2013/14.

If you're in business, whatever structure your business uses, you, personally, will have to fill in a self-assessment tax return for each tax year. For directors of active limited companies this will include your salary and dividend income from the company for that tax year. For any other business, this will include an extract from your accounts and a note of your share of the profits, and you'll pay income tax on the profits.

There are strict deadlines for when the self-assessment tax return must be filed each year.

You have until 31st January following the end of the fiscal year to file your tax return if you do it online, or 31st October if you file a paper form. So for example, tax returns for the fiscal year 2013/14 must be in by 31st January 2015 if they're filed online, or 31st October 2014 if they're filed in paper format.

What happens if I file my tax return late?

You'll get fined!

HMRC charge an automatic £100 penalty for any tax returns that are filed even a day late. The fine used to be limited to the amount of tax you had to pay, but from January 2012 this was no longer so – so you will have to pay £100 if you file late. And the penalty ramps up the longer you leave it to file your tax return. Later filing also means HMRC have a longer window of time when they're allowed to come and visit you and "enquire into" your tax return, that is, check your books and your figures to make sure they're correct.

So in short, don't be late!

I do recommend filing your tax return online because HMRC will work out your tax for you (**www.hmrc.gov.uk/sa/file-online.htm**). You've also got an extra three months to do your return.

But don't try and file your tax return online at the last minute, i.e. the 30th or 31st January, because hundreds of people do that and HMRC's website gets jammed.

You can either fill in your figures directly into HMRC's website, or use third party software to create and file your tax return. There are some excellent software packages available for this, and many of them can be set up to talk to HMRC's website so that you can file your tax return online directly from your software. My own favourite tax return software programme is TaxCalc (**www.taxcalc.com**) which is very reasonably priced, written in plain English, and has lots of comprehensive explanations.

If you don't want to fill in your form online, you can phone your local HMRC tax office to ask for a paper form to fill in, but remember that this must be completed and with HMRC by 31st October. You'll also have to work out the tax yourself, which can be difficult.

HMRC will send you a "Notice to complete a tax return" at the start of each new fiscal year, which will have your local tax office contact information on it. Or, you can look up your tax office on HMRC's website
(**search2.hmrc.gov.uk/kbroker/hmrc/locator/locator.jsp?type=3**).

When must I pay my tax?

Income tax and class 4 National Insurance for the self-employed is always due on the same dates every year – 31st January and 31st July. But not everyone must pay on 31st July.

Let's crunch some numbers for some examples of sole trader tax payments.

If the total amount of tax and class 4 National Insurance you have to pay for a tax year is under £1,000, then it's a bit simpler:

Rosie is a self-employed seamstress. 2012/13 was the first year she was in business.

She puts her tax return into HMRC's online software and discovers that she has £400 to pay in income tax and class 4 National Insurance.

She must pay that to HMRC and file her tax return by 31st January 2014, and because her tax and NI came to less than £1,000, she won't have to pay anything more until she comes to make her payment for 2013/14, which will be due by 31st January 2015.

But when your tax and National Insurance bill exceeds £1,000, it gets a bit more complicated:

Simon is a self-employed taxi driver. 2012/13 was the first year he was in business.

He works out, using TaxCalc, that his tax bill for 2012/13 is £3,000. That includes both income tax and class 4 National Insurance.

That'll be due for payment on 31st January 2014.

But because Simon's tax bill is over £1,000, unlike Rosie's, and it's all on income that hasn't been taxed before Simon receives it (unlike employment income, which has its tax deducted before wages are paid over), Simon also has to make what HMRC call "payments on account".

This means he must pay towards his 2013/14 tax bill, in advance, on 31st January 2014 and 31st July 2014.

The amount he must pay on each of those dates is half of his 2012/13 tax liability.

So on each of those dates he must pay £1,500 – which means that the total amount he must pay on 31st January 2014 is a whopping £4,500!

The first year of business is often a trap like this and sole traders and partners can end up having to pay 1.5 years' worth of tax in one go. Make sure you put money aside for this!

When Simon eventually works out his actual tax bill for 2013/14, he finds it comes to £3,500.

He's already paid £3,000 towards that in payments on account, so on 31st January 2015 he'll only have to pay £500 more for 2013/14.

But he'll also have to make payments on account for 2014/15 – which will each be half of the previous year's tax bill, so £1,750 each.

So on 31st January 2015 he'll have a total of £2,250 to pay.

What happens if I pay too much?

HMRC will give you a refund.

In Simon's case, if his tax liability for 2013/14 had turned out to be only £2,000, because he's already paid £3,000 on account, HMRC must give him back £1,000.

He would have £1,000 to pay on account on 31st January 2015 (half of £2,000), so what would probably happen is that he would pay nothing and receive no refund, because one cancels the other out.

What tax returns do I have to fill in?

Sole traders

If you're a sole trader, you're in luck, because you only have to do one tax return a year. Your business's accounts go into the self-employed pages of your tax return. And if your business's annual sales are under £77,000 for 2012/13 (excluding VAT if your business is registered), you'll usually be able to fill in the short self-employed pages (**www.hmrc.gov.uk/forms/sa103s.pdf**). One advantage of this is that you don't have to put all your different kinds of expenses in separate boxes. You can put them all in one box together.

If your business's annual sales are over that limit then you'll need to fill in the full self-employed pages (**www.hmrc.gov.uk/forms/sa103f.pdf**).

HMRC provide useful help for how to fill in these pages, both short (**www.hmrc.gov.uk/worksheets/sa103s-notes.pdf**) and full (**www.hmrc.gov.uk/worksheets/sa103f-notes.pdf**), and if you're using specialist tax software, this will usually walk you through filling in your tax returns, including which set of pages you need to use.

Partnerships and LLPs

HMRC have said that they treat LLPs and non-limited-liability partnerships the same for tax, so they use the term "partnership" for both.

If your business is a partnership, then you'll need to fill in at least three tax returns – one for the partnership (**www.hmrc.gov.uk/forms/sa800.pdf**) and one for each partner. One of the partners must be the "nominated partner" who's responsible for completing and filing the partnership's return.

When you're filling in your tax return as a partner, you can use the short partnership pages (**www.hmrc.gov.uk/forms/sa104s.pdf**) if the partnership's only source of income is from its trade and/or from bank interest.

If the partnership's affairs are more complicated you'll have to use the full partnership pages (**www.hmrc.gov.uk/forms/sa104f.pdf**).

HMRC provide useful help for how to fill in these pages, both short (**www.hmrc.gov.uk/worksheets/sa104s-notes.pdf**) and full (**www.hmrc.gov.uk/worksheets/sa104f-notes.pdf**), and if you're using specialist tax software, this will usually walk you through filling in your tax returns, including which sets of pages you need to use.

Limited companies

A limited company is the only kind of business that pays its own tax. In all other cases, the business owner(s) pay income tax on their share of the business's profit. Limited companies pay corporation tax on their profits, and must file their own corporation tax return.

Since April 2011, for year ends that fall on or after 31st March 2010, both the payment of corporation tax and the filing of the return must be done online. You'll need to register with HMRC to use online services in order to do that (**www.hmrc.gov.uk/online/new.htm**) – which isn't the same as completing form CT41G to tell HMRC your company exists.

Corporation tax is payable 9 months and 1 day after the company's year end, so companies with a year end of 31st March must pay their corporation tax by 1st January of the following year. Watch out for your company's cash flow if it's also registered for VAT. But the corporation tax return itself doesn't have to be filed until 12 months after the company's year end.

Along with the corporation tax return, you must also send a copy of the company's accounts to HMRC.

HMRC and Companies House do have a joint filing initiative (**www.companieshouse.gov.uk/about/miscellaneous/jointFiling FAQs.shtml**) whereby you can send your company's accounts to both parties at the same time. Remember though, that Companies House need them 3 months earlier than HMRC, so don't be late!

What expenses can I include on my tax return?

When you're preparing your accounts and filling in your tax return, the profit figure that tax is paid on (which accountants call your business's "taxable profit") is basically your business's income, less its day-to-day running costs.

If a running cost can be used to reduce your business's income and form part of the taxable profit calculation, then accountants say you can claim tax relief on that cost.

But there are some costs that you can't claim tax relief on, so when you're working out your taxable profit, they must be added back.

One classic example of this is if you entertain anyone other than employees of your business. So if you take a customer out to lunch, that's entertaining, and it's a day-to-day running cost of your business, so it can go in the expenses in your profit and loss account – but HMRC say that it's a cost on which you can't claim tax relief.

Let's crunch some numbers to see how this works.

Diana is a self-employed marketing consultant. Her profit and loss account shows that she made a profit of £30,000 for the tax year 2012/13.

But when she was adding up her expenses to work out that profit, she included £500 worth of entertaining, when she took customers out for meals.

Because she can't claim tax relief on that expense, she takes her profit figure and adds back the entertaining cost to get her taxable profit.

She must pay tax on a profit figure of £30,500.

What other tricky expenses are there?

There are quite a lot!

HMRC's rule of thumb is that your business can only claim tax relief on genuine business costs. So anything that's not related to your business doesn't qualify for tax relief. Accountants also describe these costs as "disallowable for tax".

Let's look at some classic examples.

Travel

Nearly all of us have to travel on business at some point or another.

There are a lot of complicated rules surrounding when travel expenses are allowable for tax – and when they're not. The basic rule is that only travel that relates to your business activities is allowable. Travel between your home and your usual workplace isn't usually allowable. By convention this is usually not even included in your accounts, whereas the cost of entertaining anyone other than any employees is.

If you make a journey for business but there's also a private element to that journey, you need to work out why you chose to make the journey. If the main purpose of the journey was for business then you can usually claim the travel costs that related to that part.

Let's go back to Diana, our self-employed marketing consultant.

She travels from her home in York, where she normally works, to London, where she has several clients.

She travels to London by train and stays in a London hotel for three nights.

A three-day stay, with two nights in London, would be enough to cover all her meetings, but Diana decides to take advantage of being in London to see *The Mousetrap* and have afternoon tea at Brown's Hotel. The third night of her stay relates to this, so she can only claim tax relief on two nights' accommodation, not three.

Because the purpose of her journey was business, she can claim the full cost of her train fares.

Mileage: sole traders and partners

If you travel by car on business, you can usually claim tax relief on the cost of that journey.

Home-to-work journeys almost certainly won't count as business travel.

The simplest method to use is often to add up all your business miles and multiply that figure by HMRC's approved mileage allowance payment rate, or AMAP. As from 5th April 2011 that's 45p per mile for the first 10,000 miles you travel in the fiscal year, and 25p per mile thereafter. The business doesn't actually have to pay you back for all this mileage for you to be able to claim tax relief on all of it.

But you can only work out the cost of business travel in your own car that way if your business is eligible to use the simplified accounting method, whether or not it actually does use that method that way if your business's annual sales are under the current VAT registration threshold – that's £77,000 from 1st April 2013. It doesn't matter whether your business is actually registered for VAT. HMRC just use the same limit for convenience.

If your business's annual sales are more than that figure, you have to add up all your car's running costs (fuel, servicing, MOT, repairs, insurance, tax, etc.) and then keep a log of your mileage, both business and private.

You'll then need to work out what percentage of your travel was on business, and claim that amount only of your car's running costs.

So if you travelled 6,000 business miles in the year, and 4,000 private, then you can claim 6/10 = 3/5 of your car's running costs in your accounts for that year.

If you're using this method and you buy a new car, you can also claim capital allowances (see below) on the cost of the new car, but you have to multiply the allowance by the business use percentage too.

You can't claim capital allowances if you're using the AMAP method to calculate your mileage cost.

Mileage: limited companies

Here's where the fun really starts.

If you're employed by a limited company, there's the question of who owns the car – you or the company.

If the company owns the car, that's a non-cash benefit it's providing to you and there will be extra tax to pay. The whole issue of company cars is so thorny that it would make an extra book on its own, so I'm going to steer clear of it here and assume that you, personally, own the car.

In that case, you can claim back from the company the cost of your business journeys made. By far the simplest way to do this, from a tax point of view, is to use the AMAP amounts as laid down by HMRC (**www.hmrc.gov.uk/budget2011/tiin6310.pdf**).

As from 5th April 2011 that's 45p per mile for the first 10,000 miles you travel in the fiscal year, and 25p per mile thereafter. This counts as money that the company can pay you back for expenses you've incurred personally, on behalf of the company. The company can then also claim tax relief on the amount of mileage you've claimed.

Business use of home

If you run your business from home, there is a large grey area around how much you can claim tax relief on as running costs of your home.

For limited companies and LLPs, the situation is even more complicated because the property will belong to one of the directors/partners, not to the company/LLP itself, and the company/LLP has its own legal identity. So in effect the director/partner is charging rent to the company/LLP for the use of the property – and that would count as rental income for the director/partner to declare on his/her tax return! If you're in this situation, ask your accountant to help you draw up a rental agreement.

If you're a sole trader, or a partner in a non-limited-liability partnership, you can usually claim tax relief on part of your household running costs, depending on how much you use your home for business.

We'll use Diana as an example again.

Of the eight rooms in her house (excluding the hall and bathroom), she uses two for business. Her office is used for business 90% of the time and, though her lounge is mainly used for leisure, she uses it for business 20% of the time because she sometimes greets clients in that room and gives them coffee there.

> ## Tip
>
> It's not a good idea to try and claim a room is used 100% for business, because HMRC could try to charge you capital gains tax on that room if and when you sell your home. For example, my own home office doubles up as my music room. It's where I keep, and play, my piano.

Diana adds up her home running costs. She can include:

- Mortgage interest payments (but not capital)
- Council tax
- Electricity and gas
- Water rates
- Insurance

Let's say this all came to £2,400 in 2012/13.

Diana would then divide that by 8 because she has eight rooms in her house, which makes £300. She can claim 90% of £300 for her office and 20% of £300 for her lounge. That means she can claim a total of £330 for business use of her home.

Do I have to use that method to work out the business use of my home?

No. HMRC say you can use any reasonable method, such as floor space of different rooms. Be prepared to show an HMRC inspector your calculations and to explain why you've used the method you've chosen.

If you are eligible to use the simplified accounting method as from April 2013 (whether or not you are actually using this method), you can, instead of working out the actual costs of running your business from home, opt to put in a flat monthly allowance instead.

How much you can claim depends on how many hours you spend working from home each month, as follows:

- 25-50 hours per month: £10
- 51-100 hours per month: £18
- 101 hours or more per month: £26

That's running costs. What about equipment my business buys?

As well as day-to-day running costs, HMRC let your business claim tax relief on the cost of its new equipment, its new assets such as computers and furniture, using what they call "capital allowances".

What counts as an asset?

Unfortunately there are no hard and fast rules. HMRC haven't set a de minimis limit as to how much something has to cost before it does count as an asset. My own view is that it depends on your business's size and on the asset itself. For example, for a self-employed web designer, a new MacBook Pro would be an asset, a battery pack probably would not.

It also depends on how long the item will be useful to your business. If it'll be useful for more than a year, it's probably an asset. If it's only going to last a couple of months, it's more likely to be a day-to-day running cost that comes straight off your business's income in the profit and loss account.

How do I work out my business's capital allowances?

This can get complicated so I do recommend you speak to an accountant if your business has a lot of assets. If it just has one or two, the calculation is a bit more straightforward – but only a bit.

Newly bought assets

Briefly, for most assets bought after 1st January 2013, there's an annual investment allowance of £250,000 available. This limit has been increased from £25,000 a year, for two years only.

This means that for most assets your business buys, so long as it doesn't spend more than £250,000 in the financial year (for limited companies) or the fiscal year (other businesses) on assets, the full cost of the asset can be set against your business's profit before the tax figure is calculated.

But if you're not preparing accounts to 31st December each year, then because this is a change in the rate, you have to work out how much allowance you get for the dates you're preparing accounts for.

For example, if you prepare accounts to 5th April each year, for the year ended 5th April 2013 you'll have an annual investment allowance of £81,250, worked out like this:

(£25,000 x 9/12) + (£250,000 x 3/12) = £81,250

For the year to 5th April 2014, this all falls within the period where the £250,000 limit will operate, so you can spend up to £250,000 on qualifying assets in that year and have 100% tax relief.

But the tax year to 5th April 2015 again straddles a change in rate, so for this tax year, you have an annual investment allowance of £193,750, worked out like this:

(£250,000 x 9/12) + (£25,000 x 3/12) = £193,750

Let's go back to Diana, who prepares accounts to 5th April each year.

She buys a new computer for her business on 30th March 2013, which costs £5,000 excluding VAT. This is well within the annual investment allowance figure so she can claim 100% tax relief on this asset.

If Diana is registered for VAT, then she would use the VAT-exclusive figure to claim annual investment allowance on, because she can reclaim the VAT from HMRC so she can't have the allowance on that.

If she's not registered for VAT, she can't reclaim the VAT she paid on the computer and so she would use the VAT-inclusive figure to claim the annual investment allowance.

If the asset had cost less than £2,000 including VAT and Diana had been using the flat rate scheme, then she would also use the VAT-inclusive figure for her annual investment allowance, because in those circumstances she can't reclaim the VAT.

But because Diana is registered for VAT and the asset cost over £2,000, she uses the VAT-exclusive figure of £5,000 for her allowance.

She would put this into the "annual investment allowance" box on her tax return and pay tax on a profit figure of £5,000 less.

She has claimed 100% of the value of the asset in one year, so she can't claim any more tax relief on the cost of that asset in future years.

She must also make sure that the £5,000 has not also been put into the "expenses" area of her tax return, as this would mean she is twice claiming tax relief for the same cost – which is not allowed!

Tax saving tip

Because the allowance runs on a financial/fiscal year basis, it's often a good idea to buy a new asset just before the end of that time, so around the end of March, if you have spare annual investment allowance for that year, because if you don't use your allowance each year, it's lost.

If you prepare your accounts to 31st March (or 5th April for non-limited companies) each year, you'll also be able to put the cost of the asset against your business's profit a year earlier if you buy the asset on, say, 29th March than if you buy it on 7th April.

Make sure though, that your business needs the asset anyway. Don't let the tax tail wag the business dog!

Some assets, though, are not covered by the annual investment allowance, and their capital allowances are dealt with differently. Cars are the classic example of this.

If you're a sole trader, and you've bought a car that you're going to partly use in the business, you need to decide how you're going to claim tax relief on your business use of the car.

If you're claiming business mileage, then you can't claim capital allowances on your car at all.

But if you're claiming actual cost, then you need to work out your business proportion of use of the car, as we saw earlier, then claim capital allowances on the car's cost, multiplied by the business proportion.

Lucy is a self-employed pet sitter, who prepares accounts to 5th April each year. She travels in her car to collect caged animals such as rabbits and guinea pigs from their owners, and return them at a later date.

Because she has to have a large car in order to be able to fit hutches in its boot, she has decided to claim the business proportion of her actual motoring costs, rather than claiming mileage, because the mileage rate is lower than she believes her car costs to run.

She buys a new car for £24,000 on 1st June 2013. Her business use of the car is 75% so this makes £18,000 on which she could claim capital allowances.

Because she has some personal use of the car, she can claim capital allowances at what HMRC call the "main pool rate", which is 18%.

She takes her £18,000 and multiplies that by 18%, giving £3,240 that she can claim for the tax year ended 5th April 2014.

That leaves £18,000 - £3,240 = £14,760 as her "written down value", which is the amount that she can claim tax relief on in future years for the car.

For the tax year to 5th April 2015 she will be able to claim 18% of the written down value as at the start of the tax year, so £14,760 x 18% = £2,656.80

She must then subtract that from her written down value to give the new written down value for the next tax year: £14,760 - £2,656.80 = £12,103.20

For the tax year to 5th April 2016 she can claim 18% of £12,103.20... and so it goes on.

Selling assets

If you sell an asset that you've previously claimed an allowance on, you have to check to see how much you've claimed already on that asset, and whether that amount, subtracted from what you bought the asset for, is more or less than its selling price.

Confused? Let's illustrate with some numbers.

Diana sells her computer on 1st January 2014, for £3,000.

She has already had an annual investment allowance of £5,000 on it, which was the total amount she bought it for. The amount of allowances she's already claimed, subtracted from the amount she paid for the asset, is £0 - £5,000 cost less £5,000 allowance. That's less than what she has earned by selling the asset.

If you're claiming annual investment allowance and you sell an asset then this is always going to be what's happened – the balance of what you haven't claimed against the cost of the asset will be lower than what you earn by selling it.

So Diana must pay what's called a "balancing charge" on the sale price of £3,000, which means she must add this to the amount of profit she's going to pay tax on.

Older assets

There has been an annual investment allowance available since 1st April 2008 (for limited companies), or 6th April 2008 (for other businesses), so most assets bought after that date would have been available for 100% tax relief.

If you have any older assets please see **www.hmrc.gov.uk/capital-allowances/plant.htm** for more information about how to claim tax relief on these.

And what about money I take out of my business?

You'll want to take money out of your business at some point. The tax consequences of that depend on your business structure.

If you're a sole trader, partnership or LLP, then taking money out of your business has no effect at all on the amount of tax you pay.

Yes, you did hear that right.

Because legally there's no difference between you and the business; money that you take out of your business doesn't go into your profit and loss account as an expense.

It's put into your accounts as "drawings", which are part of the capital account in the bottom half of your balance sheet. The total figure "capital account", which you saw in the example balance sheet, is money you put into the business, less money you took out, plus profit made by the business.

The same goes for personal costs that you pay for using your business bank account. They're drawings too. There are no tax consequences of drawings. You don't pay income tax on them. You pay income tax on the profit made by your business, and drawings don't come off that.

But if your business is a limited company, it's a bit more complicated.

There are three ways you can take money out of the business as a limited company director and shareholder:

1. The company can pay you a salary for the work you do.

2. It can pay you dividends on your shares in the company.

3. And it can pay you back any money you have lent to the company, which includes money you spent on the company's behalf, for example, when you buy a train ticket using a personal credit card.

And that's it.

If you take out more than the company owes you, you could risk paying extra tax!

This is one reason why it's a good idea to work with an accountant if you're running your business through a limited company.

***

The UK's tax system is very complex, and unless your business is very simple and small, I would recommend you engage an accountant to help you fill in your tax returns, particularly – and I make no apology for saying this again – if your business is a limited company.

In chapter 6 we'll look at why else you might need an accountant and how to choose a good one.

Chapter 6.

Do I need an accountant?

Some small business owners are lucky enough to have an accountant whom they trust as an adviser and who they wouldn't be without. Others pay astronomical fees and don't seem to get much in the way of help from their accountants.

Why might I need an accountant?

- A good accountant will give you peace of mind that your business's tax affairs are in proper order. This is not to be underestimated, particularly when you think what a wilderness the UK's tax system is.

- Having your accounts and tax return prepared professionally provides additional security if you want to borrow money, or go into a joint venture with another business. Some lenders may want to see accounts prepared by a qualified accountant[14] before they'll consider lending you any cash.

- A good accountant will also act as your agent with HMRC and field any awkward queries, and be at your side if HMRC visit for an inspection.

- A good accountant will understand why you're in business, and advise and charge you appropriately. If your business is a hobby

---

[14] This isn't the same as "audited" accounts. Only large businesses, and some charities, legally need to have their accounts audited – and it isn't cheap!

business and your accountant tries to push you into forming a limited company, alarm bells should start ringing.

How should I go about choosing an accountant?

Be careful, because anyone can call him or herself an accountant. It's not like a doctor or a solicitor. The term "accountant" is not legally protected, which is why bookies can call themselves "turf accountants"!

Some people say that you should always look for a qualified accountant, because more detailed descriptions such as "Chartered Accountant" are legally protected, so you can't call yourself a "Chartered Accountant" unless you really are one[15].

If you want to find a qualified accountant, look for an accountant with the following letters after his/her name:

- ACA / FCA (these are Chartered Accountants)

- ACCA / FCCA (Chartered Certified Accountants or Certified Accountants for short)

- ACMA / FCMA (Chartered Management Accountants)

The "F" rather than the "A" at the beginning of the prefix means the accountant has been qualified for longer, usually over 10 years.

These qualifications are issued by the three main accounting bodies, ICAEW (**www.icaew.com**) (or ICAS (**www.icas.org.uk**) in Scotland), ACCA (**www.accaglobal.com**) and CIMA (**www.cimaglobal.com**).

---

[15] Yes, I really am.

What are the differences between these qualifications?

Accountants who are qualified ACMA or FCMA tend to have more experience working with larger businesses. Some ACAs and FCAs think that ACCA / FCCAs are poor relations. I don't agree with that!

You might also find accountants with the letters MAAT or FMAAT after their names. These are Accounting Technicians (**www.aat.org.uk**). The Technician qualification is less in-depth than the other three.

Why should I choose a qualified accountant?

Qualified accountants must have professional indemnity insurance, so if you sue them, their insurance should cover it and you should get your money.

If the accountant makes a serious error, then you have recourse to appeal to their professional body if they're qualified.

But choosing an accountant is not as simple as thumbing through the Yellow Pages and picking a qualified accountant. There are plenty of bad qualified accountants and plenty of really good unqualified accountants. My boss in practice was unqualified and he is an excellent accountant!

What makes a good accountant?

First and foremost, look for an accountant who can speak plain English. It's your business, you're responsible for it to HMRC and potentially also Companies House, so it's vital that you understand what's going on in the finances. If you don't understand what your accountant's talking about, don't be shy – ask them to explain further. If you still don't understand, find another accountant!

Look for accountants who charge fixed fees, rather than charging by the hour. That way you avoid any nasty surprises in the shape of unexpectedly large bills. Does the fee include software for you to use to keep your books (see chapter 4) – and, even more importantly, will it cover training for the accountant to teach you to use this software?

And while we're on the subject of bookkeeping software, does the accountant offer software that's suitable for your business? Lots of accountants love Sage 50, which is great for some businesses, but don't let them give you Sage 50 if your business is very small and simple, or if you don't know double entry bookkeeping. If you're in that situation, Sage 50 will be a sledgehammer to crack a walnut!

Is the accountant experienced in your type of business, either because they've worked in that industry themselves, or have lots of clients in that field? For example, when I had my own practice, Home Business Accountant, I worked from home myself, and only took on clients who also worked from home, because I had first-hand experience of their issues.

Is the accountant forward-looking? The world is going online. Will your accountant be left behind? Do they have a good website with up-to-date tax tips and advice, written in plain English? If their website is written in accounting-speak then they will probably speak accounting-speak at you!

Look for an accountant who has good contacts. Many accountants will be able to link you up with a good bank manager, solicitor, or independent financial adviser (IFA). Accountants are very seldom allowed to help advise you about investments and pensions, which is why you may also need an IFA.

And look for an accountant who's happy to act as your agent with HMRC, so that they will speak to HMRC directly if any queries crop up in your tax affairs. This will save you having to deal with HMRC yourself. Your accountant will give you a form to fill in for this, or they may be able to file it online.

What's the best way to find a good accountant?

Ask your business contacts for a recommendation. If this isn't an option, you could try the "Find an accountant" options on the ICAEW, ACCA, CIMA and AAT websites.

Or, if you're using a desktop or online software package to do your accounts, many of them have lists of accountants who use that software with their clients.

Chapter 7.

Planning for the future

"Budgeting was a crucial innovation as the company grew. I could no longer keep everything in my head in terms of what I could afford to spend on what."[16]

You've heard about keeping your books for what's happened in the past. What about the future?

It's important to try and work out what your business is going to do in the future, both in terms of what profit it will earn and how much cash it will bring in. This can be difficult – after all, you are not Mystic Meg! But forecasting your numbers isn't about predicting them accurately down to the last penny.

"The only certainty about a forecast is that it will be wrong!"[17]

The aim of creating a forecast for your business is to make sure it has enough money coming in to go where you want it to go.

Remember, why are you in business?

Do you want to start trading overseas? Take on a new employee? Rent office space? Give your customers longer to pay you? Start using a new, more expensive supplier?

When do you want to do that?

If you plan your numbers, you'll have an idea when you'll be able to realise your ambitions for your business.

---

[16] Liz Jackson and Mick Spain, *Start Up!*, ISBN 978-0-273-70602-1 (Pearson Education Ltd).

[17] Jeremy Hope, *Reinventing the CFO*, ISBN 978-1-59139-945-2 (Harvard Business School Press).

The other good reason to plan your numbers, if you're a sole trader or in partnership, is that if you know your profits are going to go down, you can apply to HMRC to pay less tax on account (**www.hmrc.gov.uk/sa/forms/sa303.pdf**).[18]

OK, you've convinced me. How do I put a forecast together?

Every business is very different. But here's an example which gives you some general guidance for what to think about when you're forecasting, and a sample set of forecasts. We've all heard that "past performance is not necessarily a guide to the future and your investments may go down as well as up". But the past is often a good pointer to where your customers might come from in the future.

Case study

Vicky Duffield runs Tots Teas (**www.totsteas.co.uk**), a company that caters for children's parties.

When she forecasts how much profit she might make in the coming months, she looks at what's happened in the recent past.

Who are the children whose birthday parties she has catered for before? Their parents may well ask her to come back and do another party next year. She can put that in when she's forecasting her sales.

Who were the other children who came to those parties? Their parents might also decide to have their children's parties catered by Vicky.

As she books parties, she asks her customers how they heard of her, and works out how many new customers, on average, are referred by existing customers.

---

[18] See chapter 5 for more on reducing payments on account. Be careful though, if you reduce them too far HMRC will charge you interest!

She'll also look at other sources of new business, such as adverts, or flyers in her local newspaper.

Then she'll draw up a sales forecast, showing what income she thinks her business might earn over the next year.

She'll add this together and put it on her profit and loss account forecast, where she'll also put what day-to-day running costs she thinks her business will have.

As she takes on more customers, she'll have to spend more on travelling, cookery ingredients, and utensils. For example, if a child asks for a cake in an unusual shape, Vicky will need to buy a new cake mould.

Finally, Vicky considers her cashflow. Will all her customers pay on the day, or should she allow for laggards? Remember: profit and cash are not the same figure, and without cash in the bank, Vicky can't buy what her business needs.

Let's take the example of a business like Vicky's, and look at its sales forecast, profit and loss forecast, and cashflow forecast.

1) Sales forecast

This is a sample sales forecast for a business like Vicky's, prepared using a spreadsheet.

Princess Parties Catering
Sales Forecast for the year ended 31st March 2014

	April £	May £	June £	July £	August £	September £	October £	November £	December £	January £	February £	March £	Total £
Parties													
Repeat bookings	200	200	300	300	150	100	200	400	500	100	200	200	2,850
New customers by source:													
Referrals	50	50	60	60	60	70	70	60	80	40	40	50	690
Advertising	55	55	66	66	66	77	77	66	88	44	44	55	759
Flyer	41	41	50	50	50	58	58	50	66	33	33	41	569
Subtotal - parties	346	346	476	476	326	305	405	576	734	217	317	346	4,868
Cakes													
Wedding	0	45	135	180	180	90	45	0	180	0	0	45	900
Christening	30	60	30	90	30	30	60	30	90	0	30	30	510
Anniversary	60	60	30	30	60	60	30	30	30	30	60	30	510
Subtotal - cakes	90	165	195	300	270	180	135	60	300	30	90	105	1,920
Total sales	436	511	671	776	596	485	540	636	1,034	247	407	451	6,788

The business owner has added up how much she expects to make in sales each month.

She's divided these into parties and cakes, so that she has some idea of where her income will come from.

She's also added up the total sales she expects to make in a year. This will help her see if she's anywhere near needing to register for VAT. Her business deals with the general public, so she'd want to avoid this as long as possible.

Thankfully, at £6,788, her annual turnover is so small that she doesn't need to worry about that for some time yet, even if she expects a really big month in April 2014.

She then transfers the total sales line to her profit and loss forecast.

2) Profit and loss forecast

Here is her profit and loss forecast.

Princess Parties Catering
Profit and Loss Forecast for the year ended 31st March 2014

	April £	May £	June £	July £	August £	September £	October £	November £	December £	January £	February £	March £	Total £
Sales per forecast	436	511	671	776	596	485	540	636	1,034	247	407	451	6,788
Expenses:													
Ingredients	131	153	201	233	179	145	162	191	310	74	122	135	2,036
Cooking utensils	65			116	89		81			37			389
Containers and tubs	35	41			48	39		51				36	249
Laundry	11	13	17	19	15	12	13	16	26	6	10	11	170
Mileage	17	20	27	31	24	19	22	25	41	10	16	18	272
Advertising	9	10	13	16	12	10	11	13	21	5	8	9	136
Printing			20		20			15		24		21	100
Accountancy				200									200
Total expenses	268	238	278	615	386	225	289	311	398	156	157	231	3,552
Forecast profit / (loss)	168	274	392	161	209	259	251	325	636	91	250	220	3,237

The business owner has added to this sheet the sales from her sales forecast.

She's also added up how much she expects her monthly costs to be, and worked out her expected profit or loss each month and for the whole year, by taking the costs away from her sales.

She expects to make a small profit each month and for the year. Because this figure is under the personal allowance figure (£9,440 for 2013/14), unless she has any other income, she won't pay any tax.

She also needs to plan her cashflow, as she wants to buy a new cooker, so she puts together a cashflow forecast.

3) Cashflow forecast

Finally, our business owner forecasts her cashflow.

Princess Parties Catering
Cashflow Forecast for the year ended 31st March 2014

	April £	May £	June £	July £	August £	September £	October £	November £	December £	January £	February £	March £	Total £
Receipts													
Income from sales	404	474	591	723	686	540	512	588	835	641	327	429	6,749
Loan from parents			700										700
Total receipts	404	474	1,291	723	686	540	512	588	835	641	327	429	7,449
Payments													
Ingredients	131	153	201	233	179	145	162	191	310	74	122	135	2,036
Cooking utensils	65	0	0	116	89	0	81	0	0	37	0	0	389
Containers and tubs	35	41	0	0	48	39	0	51	0	0	0	36	249
Laundry	14	11	13	17	19	15	12	13	16	26	6	10	172
Advertising	17	20	27	31	24	19	22	25	41	10	16	18	272
Printing	9	10	13	16	12	10	11	13	21	5	8	9	136
Accountancy					200								200
New equipment				700									700
Total payments	271	236	254	1,112	571	228	287	293	388	152	153	209	4,154
Net cash in / (out)	**133**	**238**	**1,037**	**-389**	**115**	**312**	**225**	**295**	**447**	**489**	**174**	**220**	**3,294**
Starting bank balance	384	517	755	1,791	1,402	1,517	1,829	2,054	2,348	2,795	3,283	3,458	384
Closing bank balance	**517**	**755**	**1,791**	**1,402**	**1,517**	**1,829**	**2,054**	**2,348**	**2,795**	**3,283**	**3,458**	**3,678**	**3,678**

She looks at her profit and loss account, and works out when she expects her customers to pay her.

She takes a 50% deposit at the time of booking, which is usually a month in advance, and then 50% at the time of the party. She works this out and puts it in the "Income from sales" line.

Her laundry and accountancy costs are paid a month in arrears, that is, she pays the laundress and the accountant a month after the date of their bills to her. So, for example, she puts March's laundry cost from her profit and loss account into April on the cashflow forecast, April's into May, and so on.

All her other costs are paid immediately.

Her mileage is not cash that her business pays out. It's an expense she can put in to claim tax relief in her profit and loss account. So that doesn't go in here.

Her parents offer her an interest-free loan of £700 to buy her new cooker, which she accepts. This money arrives in her bank account in June 2013, and so she adds that to her receipts, on a separate line. As an aside, because this isn't part of her business's income, it won't be shown in her profit and loss account, and therefore won't be taxed – but it increases the money she has in her bank account, which is why she must put it here.

She buys the cooker in July 2013, so that goes in as part of her payments. Because it's a large item of equipment, an asset, this won't appear in her profit and loss account.

Then finally she adds up the total money coming in or going out for the month, by taking the payments away from the receipts.

She works out how much money she will have in the bank at the end of each month, by taking her starting bank balance for that month (the same as the previous month's ending bank balance), and adding on how much came in and went out during the month.

That gives her ending bank balance for the month.

This looks a healthy business as far as cashflow goes. There is enough money coming in to meet the business's costs.

What tools are available for forecasting?

You can use spreadsheets like the samples, if you're comfortable with using spreadsheets.

Unlike day-to-day accounts and bookkeeping, there isn't much speciality software available online for smaller businesses. I've had good experiences with Sage Forecasting (**shop.sage.co.uk/forecasting.aspx**), but remember I'm an accountant and Sage was designed for accountants!

How long should I forecast for at a time?

I'd recommend a year at most. Beyond that you're getting into the realms of fantasy, Jones.

Once my forecast for the year is done, can I change it?

Absolutely yes. For example, if our business owner finds out in January that one of her customers' older siblings is going to be confirmed in June and would like a special party, she'll revise her forecast to include that party. This is because she would plan not only for the extra income it'll bring in, but also for the extra costs, such as different decorations for the cake.

So do review your forecast regularly and be prepared to change it. Don't stick rigidly to it in the face of common sense!

The End

Thank you for reading this book.

I hope it's given you some help with the finance and accounting side of running your business.

During my career I've met a lot of people who begin by being really worried about 'doing the books', because they're concerned that if they put so much as one toe out of line, HMRC will be down on them like a ton of bricks.

While the UK's tax system is a jungle, it is possible to find your way through it and keep your tax affairs simple, and I hope I've given you a map and compass in this book, so that at least you know where to find the help you need.

Don't let a fear of 'the numbers' put you off starting or growing your business. I've known small business owners make comments like "I feel liberated, I didn't know it was going to be so easy", once they have the right tools to use.

Good luck, go forth and calculate!

Bibliography

James Smith BSc ACA, *Tax Guide – Keeping it Simple – Small Business Bookkeeping, Cash Flow, Tax and VAT*, ISBN 978-1-907302-16-9 (Taxcafe UK Ltd)

Hugh Williams FCA, *Proper Coffee and Other Ways to Grow Your Business*, ISBN 1-904053-86-6 (Lawpack Publishing Ltd, 2005)

Wendy Pascoe, *Starting a Business in the Country*, (How To Books Ltd)

Emma Jones, *Working 5 to 9: How to Start a Successful Business in Your Spare Time*, ISBN 978-1-906-65968-4 (Harriman House Ltd, 2010)

Steve Parks, *Start Your Business Week by Week*, ISBN-13 978-0-273-69447-2 (Pearson Education Ltd)

Liz Jackson and Mick Spain, *Start Up!*, ISBN 978-0-273-70602-1 (Pearson Education Ltd)

Emma Jones, *Spare Room Start Up: How to Start a Business from Home*, ISBN 978-1-905-64168-0 (Harriman House Ltd, 2008)

Jeremy Hope, *Reinventing the CFO*, ISBN 978-1-59139-945-2 (Harvard Business School Press)

Other Products from Enterprise Nation

www.enterprisenation.com/bookshop

GET THE BEST SUPPORT FOR YOUR SMALL BUSINESS

Join **Enterprise Nation**

A thoroughly modern business club

- Free business eBooks

- Discounts on business events

- Exclusive business benefits – including access to over 1,000 workspaces in 85 countries

Enterprise Nation helps thousands of people turn their good ideas into great businesses.

We also represent your views in the heart of government.

So, take your business to the next level – with comprehensive support, including marketing help, networking opportunities and over £500-worth of exclusive business benefits.

Join the club now for just £20 per year – and get a FREE Enterprise Nation mug!

Find out more at **www.enterprisenation.com**.